Images of Women in Transition

Images of Women in Transition

Compiled by Janice Grana

Saint Mary's Press
Christian Brothers Publications
Winona, Minnesota

The publishing team included Carl Koch, FSC, development editor; Mary Duerson Kraemer, copy editor; Barbara Bartelson, production editor and typesetter; Evy Abrahamson, cover designer and illustrator; pre-press, printing, and binding by the graphics division of Saint Mary's Press.

Published 1991 by Saint Mary's Press, 702 Terrace Heights, Winona, MN 55987-1320.

Printed in the United States of America

Printing: 6 5 4 3 2

Year: 1997 96 95 94 93 92

ISBN 0-88489-272-7

Contents

Foreword

To be human is to be conscious. Life is full of surprises, those that elate us and those that bring us to despair. Surprises may come in the beauty of a rainbow in a rain-filled sky or in a child's question, "How do you talk to God?" They may come in the shame of a hurtful statement, in the "glory" of a love relationship, in the challenge to identify and respond to God's call to ministry, or in the disappointment and despair when structures are unresponsive to profound human need.

To be human is to be fully alive and present to those unrepeatable moments experienced alone and within relationships.

To be human is to theologize. As you read this book, you will discover that women can and are doing theology. Theologizing involves thinking about Ultimate things; developing a deeper awareness of the ideas, the feelings, and the events that shape our life; confronting our own life; seeking meaning and fulfillment in our daily living; acting on our convictions and reflecting on their outcomes.

Thus, *experience* is at the center of much of women's theology. In increasing numbers, we are finding that our experience can be trusted as valid and authenticating. We discover theology reflected in our histories, struggles, commitments, and celebrations.

Women's theologizing will always be personal, but it will not be private. Appropriating our experience is ofttimes a frightening event: a painful struggle requiring sisterhood and mutual support of other women and men. The writing, singing, and living we do may not look like the patriarchal theologizing of the past, but it will be consistent with what we experience and will give shape and structure to our lives.

We are beginning to claim the reality of our experience with a new sense of urgency. For those of us who choose to live and work and grow within the framework of the Church, that urgency is particularly real. Reclaiming the participation of women from the past introduces us to strong women who walked the way before us—women like Miriam and Deborah, Sojourner Truth and Anne Hutchinson, the witches and the saints.

The developing theology of women promises new life to the intellectual detachment found too often in the Church today. Women proclaim hope and a belief in the future as our own basis for remaining in a Church so desperately in need of revolution and rebirth.

For the pioneering women embarking on theological journeys today, life will not wait. In their lives, these women are dedicated to the hope of claiming a future filled with self-respect and dignity. For the present, there are no resting places, no comfortable or secure paths, no maps to guide us. But the journey has begun. The personal experiences and insights in this book reveal the becoming process of movement and discovery. And having set our faces, our very lives, toward the Light, there can be no turning back.

Sharon Zimmerman Rader

Preface

The idea for this book originated with the Upper Room staff in dialog with Nan Self of the Commission on the Status and Role of Women, The United Methodist Church. We sensed a need among women to write about their personal experiences from a context of change, struggle, and sometimes frustration. The publication of these women's concerns and expressions was seen as a means of women listening to and communicating with one another. The suggestion became the working proposal for *Images*.

A short news release was printed that invited Christian women to share their own stories: searches for identity, spirit struggles, vocational commitments, celebrations, and challenges. The staff circulated the invitation through newspapers and special mailings. I was certainly unprepared for the response. Within a short time, manuscripts from all across the country poured in. Eventually material from more than six hundred women was received and screened.

As I read the manuscripts, varied as they were, I began to realize how important this project was! The excitement and expectation generated by the book revealed a deep desire among women to tell their own stories and learn the concerns of other women. Through letters and telephone calls, I was caught up in the spontaneity and the full impact of what was taking place as these Christian women started to put into words their explorations and insights, sometimes out of deeply painful experiences.

The process of reading and responding to the material was a significant personal experience. I came face-to-face with women who were willing to risk being honest in the midst of complexity, and to accept themselves and their possibilities. Above all, I was conscious of a genuine search for wholeness and growth, combined with a sensitivity to the needs of others. As I shared in their moments of self-discovery, I came to a new awareness of my own feelings and concerns. Their reflections caused me to see myself more clearly.

This book is unique. It affords an in-depth understanding of women of various ages, lifestyles, interests, and religious backgrounds. Even though each woman is speaking from her own situation, the totality of the book reveals a sense of community. I believe this is possible because as individuals honestly share, a real bond links us one to the other. From such community, we can look to the future with renewed confidence and hope.

I wish to express my special appreciation to Perry MacDonald for her valuable assistance in the selection and editing process, to Nan Self for her cooperation and guidance, and to all the women who submitted material in support of the publication.

Janice Grana
World Editor
The Upper Room

A Search for New Identities

Separation Joy

Part of the gray, fluid, neutral blob
Changing shapes for different roles
Reflecting the nearest Important Person.
Somebody's daughter
Somebody's wife
Somebody's secretary
Somebody's friend
"I love you because I like who I am when I am with you."

Sunburst!
God's gift is the ME PERSON
Special and unique
Important among the Important Persons
ME being daughter
ME being wife
ME being employee and mother and friend
"Because I like who I am, I can love who you are."

Hurray!!!

Anne Trapp

A New Day

The world is clean—washed by the rain,
fresh and new, smelling of
damp earth, green grass and spring;
and I feel as if life were beginning
again for me, that like the
willows, I have renewed my bones
with fledgling leaves. My face
turned upward to welcome the rain;
and I, for all my years, am newly born,
seeing the world with wondering eyes.

Marla Visser

The Call

We are
to be
the mannequins

thin, mute,
and haughty

set before windows
to be seen
marveled at
appreciated

locked
where spots of anchored light
will fall.

Somewhere alone
wanders
the woman in me
far away from the dollar toys
and dull of window eyes.

> Come along,
> come along
> New-Born.
> I have room for you
> in the soul
> of one person
> singing.

Greta Schumm

(Written with special affection for
Queen Vashti of Esther 1:10–22)

Pedestal

Even if a prison
Is called a pedestal
And is bedecked with flowers
and flattery,
It is no less confining
or demeaning.

Margaret House Rush

What Other Song

I know I do this well—
This tending of home, this
Bearing of children, this love
To my husband, this now tame
Now wild filling a woman's function
Up to the brim and over.
This was a choice I made,
Or perhaps a role I took with love
When it was passed to me
By nature, by upbringing, and by love.
But what of that other life
I have no birth for yet
(I have no time for yet
I have no breath for yet),
That song I almost hear and cannot silence
Try as I will, knowing it costs, now,
More than I can give?
   Will it wait for me?
How long will it wait? I wonder
Who I am that half listens
Half turns away.

Martha Whitmore Hickman

Whatever Happened?

When I was a kid, I thought that although the world belonged to the adults, it was an exciting wonderland of living things waiting to be discovered, that each person in it had some unique and fascinating charm or talent to share, that if I followed the rules, the world would be good to me, and that God was indeed everywhere.

Now I complain that the world belongs to the kids, that it is a depressing confusion of crowded tenements, traffic jams, polluted streams, and reeking smog, that most people are selfish bores, that the only rules worth following are those that help me get ahead, and I'm wondering where God is in all of this.

What happened to the world?
What happened to me?

Judy K. Payne

Colors

I no longer cling to pastels.
They did for a while,
But I outgrew them.

And now I want strong colors,
Confident in their boldness,
Bright enough to stand proudly.

Pastels are too shy, too hesitant;
Unsure, not quite ready to
Plunge,
Like a prelude.
You see, pink is for deciding,
Red is for decision.

Pastels are the bud not quite ripe,
Unready to be seen.
A preview.

Now I long for the deeper hues,
The intensity of the greens.
I'm ready for the flower, full-bloom.

Adele Allen

Responsible

there is a me
what an awesome responsibility
it is easy to pass over the you they and thems
but when it comes to me
responsibility for me is held by me
that at times is awesome
sometimes it is a burden but
imagine me responsible for me
at times responsibility for others must be assumed
but me i can't give away
    i can't sell
    i can't barter
all these things are tried over and over
i will never be unemployed
i have me to take care of

Mary Eleanore Rice

Catch a Timeline

I rise above
and catch a timeline
Jetstream
north   —   south
west — east.
I cannot see it,
yet it sustains
and lifts
and thrusts me
forward into space.
So life ————
jetstreaming
between
birth
and
death.
God holding
both ends.

Murden Woods

Reflections of a Woman

What reflections will I see in God's mirror?
Will the many facets be in balanced harmony?
Or will one glaring light obscure the rest?
Will I be afraid or thrilled with what I see?
Am I brave enough to look, or should I turn away?

I remember the woman at the well who looked in depth,
But not so deep as Jesus, who saw her whole and new.
If I could look into the well, with Jesus looking too,
Would I see myself in fragments scattered here and there?
I feel I'd find in living water the person I was meant to be.

Lura Houck Carstens

Prayer for Myself

When I let go the selves that I feel others expect me to be,
     I sometimes find no one there.
But other times I find a surprising me, a me that no one could
     anticipate, but one that is uniquely right.

     God, help me to realize that this unique me is the one that you
intended me to be. Help me be as fresh in my awareness as a child.
Amen.

Cynthia J. Symonds

Call Me a Woman

I am twenty-five
And when I am called a girl
I speak like a girl;
I flirt and giggle and play dumb.
But when I remember I am a woman,
I put away childish things
And speak out, and share, and love.

I am thirty-six
And when I am called a girl
I think like a girl;
I feel incompetent
So I serve and help the men around me.
But when I remember I am a woman,
I put away childish things
And work, and create, and achieve.

I am fifty-two
And when I am called a girl
I understand like a girl;
I let others protect me from the world.
But when I remember I am a woman,
I put away childish things
And decide, and risk, and live my own life.

Nancy R. Smith

Take Time

> I do not consider myself to have fully grasped it even now. But I do concentrate on this: I leave the past behind, and with hands outstretched to whatever lies ahead I go straight for the goal—my reward the honor of my high calling by God in Christ Jesus. (Phil. 3:13–14, Phillips)

The past is over and done. What good is it to look back? It does not pay to look back unless you can profit from the experience of the past.

Recently I took time to look at myself. These are some of the questions I asked:

Who am I?

Where am I?

What am I doing for myself and the good of humankind?

Where do I hope to go?

Only you can answer these questions for you. Only I can answer these questions for me. The *now* is today. We must live it to its fullest. We must do what we really want and need to do. The possibilities of today are ours.

The future will break forth anew—*the New Age*. Will we be ready to face a new day? We must shape ourselves in the present to live in the future. We are the guides of the possibilities and potentialities of the future.

Stop, take an inventory of your life. Are you heading in the direction you want to go? Are you who you want to be?

Take time to look at yourself.

Ethelou Talbert

Self-Realization

The pain of
self-discovery
is worth
nothing
unless in finding
ourselves
we also find
each other.

Cynthia J. Symonds

Sorting Through

It's not that I'm a good person now, you see. Not even that I'm a *better* person, not even that. Instead it's just that I am
    seeing me
    being me
    liking me
    and that scary one—loving me.
    It's adventuring into vulnerability and compassion and sensitivity and being schooled by them:
    Discovering that as each becomes sharper, the inside me becomes richer, quieter, stronger, and a person with a person.
    Discovering that vulnerability, compassion, and sensitivity requires direction, boundary lines, control. Seems simple enough but the realization was slow, the mastery to be attained.
    It's honesty too. Even if it were wise to be totally honest *all* the time ("How are you?" "Just terrible, thanks."), I'm not. But, I'm learning that it always pays to be honest with the One that counts. Being honest with God, no matter how ugly it is, always is good.
    Painful perhaps, but good.

Barbara Platt

Who Am I?

I am a person
Separate from all others
Yet one with humanity.

I am a person
Different than others
Yet with a common bond.

I am a person
Having my own personal hurts
Yet feeling the hurts of others.

I am a person
Reaching out to help
And being helped in return.

I am a person of worth.

Janet B. Reynolds Gibbs

Reflections of Friends by the Sea

June: We are so bombarded every day by radically different messages about how we, as women, are to function. I don't know about you, but I've really had to do some soul-searching and reading to discover how I want to understand my purpose in life as a Christian woman.

Jenna: I'm often tempted to absorb unthinkingly from society or the Christian community the first, the loudest, or the most obviously scriptural viewpoint about who I should be or how I should act as a woman. Why do I do that? Sometimes it's the pressure of time or the pain of decision or concern about the reaction of my peers. But I am acutely aware that I can't afford to give someone else my God-given right to pattern my life. When I do, I cheat myself out of the joy and the growth that accompany being responsible for my own directions.

June: From my perspective, I don't have much sympathy with the "empty-nest" syndrome or running around volunteering, doing handicrafts, or playing bridge as a means of escape from boredom. I've tried it, and it is a very empty life. As most of my children are grown and on their own, my main purpose in life is *not* my children. Can I have a broader concept or worldview and find friends on my own? Am I ready and able for the kind of relationship that allows my husband and me to be our own kind of people?

Jenna: Even though I have children who are the ages that need my nurturing care, I don't see my purpose in life as living *for* them or *through* them. They are little people who are dependent upon others, particularly Dad and Mom, but I don't see myself using them to gain the label for myself as "super-Mother." This past year and a half, my husband has been the "house-person" and I the "breadwinner." The role change was awkward at first and initiated inadequate feelings for both of us. But the arrangement has produced within Bob a new vision, appreciation, and skills for the tedium of homemaking and the patient responsiveness needed to care for young boys. I have more confidence and strength to stand behind my viewpoints and plans. I want my boys to see that being strong and gentle are both male and female traits.

June: We do owe our children a picture of development in our own life so that they will have a becoming pattern of maturity. They must see that it isn't necessary for anyone to ever stop becoming. Changing careers at forty was a real earth-shattering experience at my home. When I had to be away for the schools, seminars, and workshops needed to learn new skills, Father and the children were *forced* to get to know one another and handle problems that came up. I had really hampered the development of all by very quietly coping and handling everything within the home. Growth only happens when we have new vision, and when we come face-to-face with God's gift of freedom.

Jenna: Becoming mature isn't easy! I see that husband and wife both have an obligation to grow *in their own uniqueness* from where they are! We must resist being stereotyped by what the other wants us to be. Coming to grips with conflict is an essential ingredient. Persons committed to each other in a marriage must be willing to endure the pain, confusion, and hurtful isolation of struggling together for alternatives. Only then can each discover the blessings that come from *building* a solution together. I feel the path to maturity is never a straight incline lined on each side with protective rails. That would allow no vision of other people's pilgrimages. To me it's more like a continuous spiral—flexing like a spring always on the move as I embrace others and the feelings of life. Is there something we can say—something uniquely female—about where we are—in *our* moment in history?

June: I'm not sure my view or what I can say is unique. I'd like to view myself as Jesus would see me—as a person created in God's image, a person God wants to be whole, to grow, to learn, to use fully my talents and gifts.

Jenna: It would be unrealistic if I didn't mention and affirm that I am a woman and rejoice in being so. I am one of the two different types of people God created. But I am not in competition with the males in my life . . . I am in commitment. That commitment is a conscious dedication to help others grow. It means challenging, comforting, laughing, and crying alongside other people. It means deliberately choosing not to *abuse* or *use* one another.

June: It's very difficult for me to just talk about the woman's role because I see that so many of the answers to life and the message of the Gospel are messages for both sexes.

Jenna: There is such a unity of purpose in being a follower of Christ that I can't ask myself: "Was that a feminine thing to do?" Rather I ask: "Was that a Christlike action of compassion and love?" I believe Galatians 3:27–28 affirms this truth: "All baptised in Christ, you have all clothed yourselves in Christ, and there are no more distinctions between Jew and Greek, slave and free, male and female, but all of you are one in Christ Jesus" (Jerusalem Bible).

June White
Jenna Shultz
(June White and Jenna Shultz are friends who took two days to share their insights and examine their lives as women in God's world.)

Images

O God, I am chained to my images—
  Daughter
    Sister
      Tomboy
        Brain
          Sweetheart
            Housewife
            Mother
              Chauffeur
              Cook
                Hostess

All of these am I? Torn?
  Disintegrated?
  Or none?
  No, I cannot deny them.
  They have become part of me.
  But somewhere,
Slipping silently between the images,

Is there someone else?
  Someone whole?
    Poet?
      Pastor?
        Mystic?
          Scholar?
            Music Maker?
              Counselor?
            Lover?
              Friend?
How shall I know?

And you, God, are you also chained and hidden
By your images, your names, your roles?
  Creator
    Judge
      Father
        Redeemer
          King
            Savior
              Christ
                Son of God
                  Holy Spirit
                  Light

Are you also lost among the images,
    Struggling to emerge into new roles,
    Fresh revelations of your real self?
Are you not also
    Poet?   Becoming?
        Artist?   Suffering?
            Mother?   Loving?
                Daughter?   Changing?
                    Mystery?   Singing?
                                Rejoicing?
                                    Darkness?
                                    Despair?

Can we emerge together, you and I?
Can we break the chains that bind us
    and move out into the fresh air of liberation?

Call me into being, God!
And let me catch a glimpse of you as you really are
    in this moment of time and eternity!

Betsy Phillips Fisher

Time

If I had a summer
to give you, my mutilated psyche,
maybe you could heal into oneness.
But always there are the things
that pull me apart,
chewing up my ego,
possessing my time and leaving me
with one small question.
When do I get to be me?

Marla Visser

Facing Women: Historical Perspectives

Just as the architecture of the past affects us today (note the Grecian columns or cathedral ceilings) and just as scientific discoveries of the past build on themselves, so too do the attitudes and traditions of our past affect our present attitudes toward people.

The past that faces women today begins with the ancient but still recited Thanksgiving Prayer repeated by the Hebrew male upon rising . . . "Blessed art thou, Lord, that thou hast not made me a woman."

The Greek view of women and motherhood is expressed as: "The mother is no parent of that which is called her child: but only nurse of the new-planted seed that grows."[1]

In the second century, the Christianity of the institutional Church did little to improve the image of women. Saint Clement wrote: "Every woman should be overwhelmed with shame at the very thought that she is a woman."[2] "Women . . . were naturally depraved, vicious, and dangerous to the salvation of men's souls—a commodity women needed not to worry about as they were possessed of none."[3]

Yet motherhood of sons was considered a sacred duty. How was a woman to deal with this sort of double image being presented her?

Menstruation and childbirth made her unclean. Monthly she was banned from entering the church, and after childbirth, if she lived, she was barred from the church for six weeks as her "sacred duty" had left her unfit. She was not even permitted to participate in the baptism of the child.

These then are some of the historical images facing women today, and these historical images become present reality. When men refuse to receive communion from a woman minister, we are hurt and angry. It is then that we become aware through pain of the need to fight the continuing oppression of our past.

We are discovering a mixed heritage—freedom as well as oppression. We are finding an identity. We are unearthing people—women people—overlooked by previous historians. In the face of ingrained (thereby unintentional) *and* intentional exclusion . . .

We find courage, strength, and hope.

Candace E. Reid

1. Elizabeth Gould Davis, *The First Sex* (Baltimore: Penguin Books, 1972), p. 187.
2. Davis, p. 231.
3. Davis, p. 241.

The Presence of God

Signatures

I scrawl my name
in mellow sand—
claiming the beach,
the sky,
the breeze,
the cry
of gulls as mine.

And while,
smiling with power,
I survey my grant,
a vagrant wave uncoils,
laps,
smudges,
quietly erasing.

God signs the Creator's name
in craggy shores,
swept sky,
mosaic seas,
and signal cries
by wheeling gulls.

No wave invalidates this document.
Each carves it more indelibly.

God, sign the barren beaches of my life.

Evelyn Minshull

Pieces

I am a million pieces: a jigsaw puzzle. I cannot move. I am helpless.
   HELP ME, GOD.
I am a thousand pieces. I am good. I am bad. I am here. I am there.
   HELP ME, GOD.
I am a hundred pieces. I am rich. I am poor. I am wise. I am foolish.
   HELP ME, GOD.
I am ten pieces. I am young. I am old. I am lovely. I am ugly.
   HELP ME, GOD. FASHION ME ACCORDING TO YOUR WILL.

Anna Purviance

The Shadow and the Real

I have been in a crowded room.
Maybe you were there, too.
We were busy talking about people and their needs—about relating
    our faith to those needs.
I had some good ideas in planning programs.
I left the room and was satisfied with my contribution.
It's easy to feel satisfied in the shadow.
I have a friend who recently observed her sixth wedding anniversary
    by herself. Her husband died this year; she has a burden of grief.
I have another friend whose husband left her with two preschool
    children and a deep sense of failure; she has a burden of loneliness.
I have another friend who is haunted by her past; she has a burden of
    guilt.
The couple who live next door to me are fulfilling their dream of
    building a new home. Yet, they are not happy; they have a burden
    of emptiness.
I met a man today who knows that he can live only another year or
    two; he has a burden of fear.

The Real seems so complicated.

God, help me today to step out of the shadow and into the Real.
The Real makes me feel so exposed and vulnerable—I may have to
    hurt some if I love enough to see people as you see them.
I prefer the security and calm of the shadow.

And Jesus said, I am The Real . . . there is no other way . . . except
    by me. If you want to be my follower, you have to step out of the
    shadow yourself and into the Real with me. Whenever you get
    involved in the lives of the people around you, you're loving me,
    too. You won't find your happiness in the shadow, but the Real will
    give you joy and peace like you've never known!

Yes, God, I hear you.
I'm glad for the gift of your Spirit and the promise that I am not alone in
*   the Real. But I'll need a reminder now and then to keep me from*
*   fading into the shadow again.*

Sheila R. Morris

Patchwork Woman

Patchwork quilt,
Woven with unsettling ambiguities and
definite victories,
My life evolves.

Fragmentation
Bound together by threads of yearning
to be a center
Centered in the beyond.

Awaken yearnings and bend the margins
on your dreams!

Margaret House Rush

Pentecost

In quietness and trust,
I yield myself this moment
To the Presence that gives me life,
To the Reality that existed before the earth was made,
To the Spirit that came and *comes* as fire
To turn around our lives
And make them new.

Burn within me, God!
Let me feel your fire!
Burn warm with love!
Burn bright with joy!
Burn hot to consume
    all that makes me doubt your power in me,
    your love through me.
Burn away my barriers to completeness.
Burn away my limited consciousness,
    inbred by habits of thought,
    by opinions of others
    by seeming necessities that have become my master.
Burn away my slavery to fear
And teach me, within,
    the looseness of listening,
    the rhythm of trust.

Grace Adolphsen Brame

The Middle-Time

Between the exhilaration of Beginning . . .
  And the satisfaction of Concluding,
    Is the Middle-Time
        of Enduring . . . Changing . . . Trying . . .
          Despairing . . . Continuing . . . Becoming.

Jesus Christ was the Human of God's Middle-Time
  Between Creation and . . . Accomplishment.
Through him God said of Creation,
  "Without mistake."
And of Accomplishment,
  "Without doubt."

And we in our Middle-Times
  of Wondering and Waiting,
    Hurrying and Hesitating,
    Regretting and Revising—
We who have begun many things . . .
  and seen but few completed—
We who are becoming more . . . and less—
Through the evidence of God's Middle-Time
  Have a stabilizing hint
    That we are not mistakes,
    That we are irreplaceable,
    That our Being is of interest,
        and our Doing is of purpose,
    That our Being and our Doing
        are surrounded by Amen.

Jesus Christ is the Completer
  of unfinished people
  with unfinished work
  in unfinished times.

May he keep us from sinking, from ceasing,
  from wasting, from solidifying,
That we may be for him
  Experimenters, Enablers, Encouragers,
  and Associates in Accomplishment.

Lona Fowler

He Comes

Christ the Lord is risen this day!
Hallelujah, Lord!

He comes to some, waiting in the cold gray dawn,
As the sun's first rays come: melting effortlessly over the horizon;
Bringing a slow rich sense of well-being
A confidence that all is well
A quiet reassurance that he is near.

Christ our Lord has risen this day—
On this Easter Day.

He comes to others,
   restless as the first fingers of light pierce the gloom of night,
As the sun itself comes: bursting forth in all its glory—a red ball of
      fire
Demanding attention
Breaking out into the dawn.
It hangs in the sky—assured
Vibrant
Prominent
Radiant in its cosmic light.
Christ comes like this to some, suddenly.
And dark is made light,
Night becomes day.
Questions seem answered.
Doubt is dispelled.
Uncertainty fades away,
And we are certain that he is Lord.

So sure, O Lord, so sure.
For Christ the Lord is risen today.
Risen! Risen!

And now the night has gone.
Where stars once broke the monotony of blackest night
A sun now moves across the sky: regal
All powerful
Never swerving from its course.

And in our lives, where little things—unimportant things—trivial
    things—
Once prevailed:
Now a Master moves.
A King
A Christ
Our Risen Lord.

Martha Edens

Bedrock

The pebbles lie about
In great profusion;
Their muted colors
Brighten with the surf.
I grab them eagerly
To feel their smoothness,
To heft them one against the other.
Some I keep for quite a while,
Clinging to their tactile substance.
Then one by one
I loosen each and let it fall.
It is not what I seek—
Not the true bedrock
After all.

But never once
Do I doubt
That the bedrock
Is there—
Somewhere.
And so,
My search continues.

Normagene Warner

Prayer Is for Real People

Prayer is
the real you
recognizing the presence
of the real God.
God has waited for you;
God has moved you to want a Holy Friend,
and you respond
in words or thoughts
or concepts,
or by just
"being"
in God's presence.

Prayer is the real you
acknowledging the real God
in spite of
your bad grammar or your lisp
or your elegant adjectives,
your self-criticism
or your "cover up,"
your intelligence
or your knowledge;
the real you,
hungry for something special
in spite of not having much to say
although your heart is full
and your brain befuddled.

Prayer is being honest, then,
"getting to the nub,"
caring about what counts.
You may wrestle;
Jacob did.
You may see a vision
a concept in a picture.

Do not put a veil between;
it will just fool *you*.
Remember God is real too
and will start just where you are,
even if you don't know where that is.
Breathe deeply!

It's a big relief
to be

just you.

Grace Adolphsen Brame

Prayer of Life

O God,
Your love warms me, draws me as a moth to its light.
Your love charms me, draws me as the music of the pied piper.
Once I embraced life—
and was cut by the sharp edges.
Bitterness poured into my wounds like salt water.
O God,
I am afraid: afraid of the sharp edges, yet longing again for the fierce
   joy of embracing life.
I yearn to shout YES again in ecstasy of abandonment to you.

Linda Felver

Awareness

I know the spirit in this mortal frame
Marked with personality and name
Can, by awareness, any given hour,
Ally itself with God. Then all the power
That floods the universe with living light
Can surge and flow through me, and lift my sight
To higher levels, hushed and glad and free,
Until I know that God is touching me.

But like a child with book or game or ball,
The span of my attention is so small!

Louise Sullivan

Circles

A pebble dropped into a pool
Makes circles widening outward.
I watch and slowly all of life
Revolves in expanding arcs.

A wedding band, for endless love,
A baby's teething ring;
Circle of firelight illumining
Loved ones as they laugh and talk.

The golden ball of a full moon
Shining on cabin roof;
Dandelion and daisy chains
Fashioned by children's hands.

Those small black circles on a staff
That magically turn to song;
And friends who sing or talk or cry
In meeting mutual needs.

These are the circles of my life
That intersect and widen.
God's purposes, like pebbles dropped,
Bring meaning to them all.

Eleanor P. Anderson

Ad Lib

No puppet, I.
Christ dissolved those strings I once obeyed
   (frenzied, collapsing, dangling in despair)
and set me free—
a freedom fraught with terror at the start:
   Am I on now?
   Was that my cue?
   Have you the script?
until his patience taught me that
there is no script—
just love and ad-libbing his praise.
No strings—
just ties.

Evelyn Minshull

Psalm of a Modern Woman

Confronted by the day, O God, I cry to thee.
I cry . . . in part;
   a hundred things to do press on my thoughts.
I cry . . . in brief;
   a schedule crammed with duties crowds me so.

Why must there be no time, no time?
Why must there be so much, so much?

My hours sink in the stove, the car, the television
I live with chrome and steel and plastic
But not with thee, O God, but not with thee.

As the hart longs for flowing streams, so longs
   my soul for thee, O God,
As the harried worker longs for peace and quiet,
   so longs my soul for thee.

Sue Nichols Spencer

All of Creation

Mountain Thoughts

1

The mountain
moves
about me in every
breath of air
that
nods
the grass or
whines
the tree.

I feel a
movement
in the air of
wings,
leaves,
and underfoot a
gentle
soft earth
movement.

A nodding flower
speaks
color
to a quiet forest
green.

I stop to rest.

Upon my face is
sun
then
shade
and sudden cold of
rain.

Subtle sounds
quiet me
in gentle chorus;
movements
that I strain to note
sharpen,
reawaken

awareness and
wonder.

Wonder
at the grandeur of
God
and the glory of the Creator's
art.

My breath flows.
My feet walk.

Suddenly
I am a
rhythm
with the wind
one
with earth and sky.
All
is whole.

The growing, living, moving,
the crumbling, withering, dying
are
one.

2

Here
there are no puzzles to be
fitted;
no solutions to be
found;
no one for me to
guide
advise.

Here
all fits and comforts me.
Chides
my searching
my planning
in some
temporary wrinkle of
time.

Below.

All is one
above
and so should be
below
if I but sense the
flow
of me and thee
within
my world
down there
below.

Stretched out within the
shadow
of the mountain
if I but lift my
eyes
if I but
listen,
the mountain speaks.

Catharine Stewart Roache

~

In God-consciousness
Not reasoned but instinctive
I am primitive.

Jean Fox Holland

Divine Whisperings

Silence was so still
  I heard my heart beat
  as I lay in the sunlight on the sand.
Looking through lattice fingers,
  I watched one sheer-green blade of grass
Beating to the rhythm of a vagrant breeze.
In mystery, the separate rhythms matched.

Edith Griswold Farey

Just a Moment Longer

God, I am confounded!
Your earth is too beautiful
To pass over lightly.
Let me pause to watch
The tide come in,
Let me linger to watch
The poinciana bloom.
Let me hold the puffs of silk cotton
Before they blow away.
Hold the fiery sun up
Just over the western waters
A moment longer,
Just a moment while I look again.
Let me hug this sleepy child
To my breast
A few more years,
A few more hours,
Just a moment more,
God.

Violet Munro

Come Out

Who wants to work on a morning like this?
Who wants to sit at a desk?
Who wants to type, or to sew, or to cook?
Or even curl up with an interesting book?
When the whole outdoors shouts.
"Come, take a look!"

And the road from here to most anywhere
Is wet from the rain and as washed as the air
And the breeze keeps patting and combing my hair,
And it whispers in urgency, "Get out of that chair.
Come out to this sunshine,
Come away from in there!"

Sophia E. Smith

Winter

winter is so beautiful
and the wintry portions of my life
are those which often give birth
to a deeper understanding of who God
created me to be
winter for me is an eye-opener
i learn to appreciate
instead of bemoaning
to delight at the sight of freshly fallen snow
looking in awe
at the frost-frozen tree limbs
openly rejoicing and celebrating
because winter gives me more time to explore
to reach out
a time to make new plans
with a new ripple of hope
within my soul.

Penny Tressler

Eventide on the Beach

The tide is ebbing now and one little star
Is faintly seen through the evening sky, though its distance is far.
As I stand on the lonely shore, I know
God guides the tides of my life that ebb and flow.

Pauline Reeder Liddle

Star Wish

In azure upturned cup of sky
Shine random stars.
Discerning their significance
We are like gypsies,
Tracing tea-leaf meanings
Of our hopes and fears.

Anita Wheatcroft

Wings

Today is a cold bleak day when one can feel spring wrestling with the chains of winter which have held the earth in a viselike grip. The many colorful birds outside my window are frantically flitting from feeder to feeder in response to the hunger signals from their tiny built-in radar systems.

And, then, after satisfying this drive to survive, they fly off into the freedom of the woods. Even as they feed, they know they have wings—wings that can lift them quickly to safety when they hear the stealthy steps of the neighborhood cat or the footfall of a person on the path. It is then they rise as a single cloud to the skies.

Just now as I write, one little purple finch dashes itself with a pounding thud against the window pane. It veers off the feeder in the wrong direction and lies seemingly lifeless in the bed of ivy, almost at my feet. As I sit and watch it panting, I find myself wanting somehow to help it, but knowing I can't. This finch is one of the lucky ones, for after several minutes I thrill to see it stir, then stagger, and finally spread its wings and lift itself skyward. It is wounded but still able to fly.

The finch is God's creation. So am I. Many days I have watched these bits of feathered loveliness and envied them their freedom from problems, envied them their wings that lift them high above the horizon.

Today I am thinking about them again and a new understanding comes that we are much alike. God has provided for our many kinds of physical needs in different ways, expecting each of us to help ourselves.

Each of us has experiences that dash us, winded and wounded to the ground, but with God's hand of courage to grasp, we can pick ourselves up and reach for the heights of life again.

God has given us wings—wings of vision, wings of hope, wings of faith, wings of courage, wings of love. We too are surrounded by God's love and care.

Mary Jane Hartman

Yet, They Bloom

There beside the road,
The Queen Anne's lace
Was meant to tower
And twist and turn
In all its grace,
Showering beauty on every landscape.
Flowers of white
In tatted loveliness.
Flowers of white
In regal finery.

Beside it there along the road
So short and stubbed
I did not recognize at first
Is white sweet clover.
Wild sweet clover meant
To be a feast
For sucking bee,
Meant to thrive and tower
Sending its intricate plumes
In every direction—
Yet—it's lower than the clods about my feet.

How many times
Has struggling Leaf
Been cut and torn?
Their ever-greening heads
Shorn and strewn along the way?
Each time they've struggled
To stand tall,
The mower blade has sheared them off.
Some roots could not withstand
The fearsome slash.
But those left—
Are stunted and dwarfed and nowhere near
What they were meant to be.
And yet they bloom!
And yet they bloom!

Normagene Warner

Creation

The indomitability of the life spirit:
    Winter night: a bird,
    Heedless of the sun's absence,
    Sings into the dark.

And the steadfastness of God's work:
    Once more wildflowers
    Splash with color roadside, fields,
    And hills—as always.

    Old earth, wrinkled, scarred,
    Has gifts for us, and wisdom.
    Our task is to learn.

Virginia K. Anderson

Free Flight

Your Easter lesson, Holy Friend,
    is not in birds and bees
    but seeds and butterflies.
Seeds lie in the ground,
    giving themselves completely in the hope
    that new life might emerge
    and appear . . . to grow.
Crawling caterpillars, fuzzy worms,
    relinquishing their slow but sure existence,
    risking all in the momentary prison of the cocoon
    for the promise of soaring
                    free
                        flight.
Holy Friend, make possible for me
    the courage of the lowly worm,
    that faith of the tiny seed.

Alma Roberts

Reflections on a Moment

The sense of power comes—not an aggressive, dominating power—but an inner strength that is empowering. The strength comes from a sense of belonging to the universe and feeling that I am important and relevant just as the insects, bobcats, maidenhair ferns, opossums, rivers, and armadillos. I guess it is a feeling of being alive and intertwined with all these forms of life. It is through this that I gain respect for nature, for creation, for the Creator. It is through God's creativity that this comes about. It is for me to continue to create—not to destroy that delicate balance of life of which we humans are only a small part.

Rare, quiet moments but coming at times when I need them most. I require these moments for living, as a life-giving self-confidence. These brief moments of trust—trust of my own emotions, my own thoughts, my own reactions. For me this is God's creativity seen in nature, God's creativity seen, felt in me—God's endless energy bounding through every creative process in which I am immersed.

That rapid, loudly pounding surge, that breath, that wind all throughout every fiber in my body when I am creating through dance or painting. Sometimes it comes as a quiet feeling that fills me when I am standing alone out by the sea, or in the forest, or by a painting. The surge comes and I reply, smiling, "I know."

Marilyn Cook Rabb

The Kiss of Spring

Who but God can rescue earth from the grip of winter?
God takes the bare fields—bleak and desolate—and
dresses them in green, splashing us with colors,
reminding us that LIFE comes through the Creator. All about
me buds are bursting. . . . I am dwarfed by God's great
universe when spring arrives.

Tammy Felton

~

All the things that are
Delight me this day. I laugh
And wiggle my toes.

Jean Fox Holland

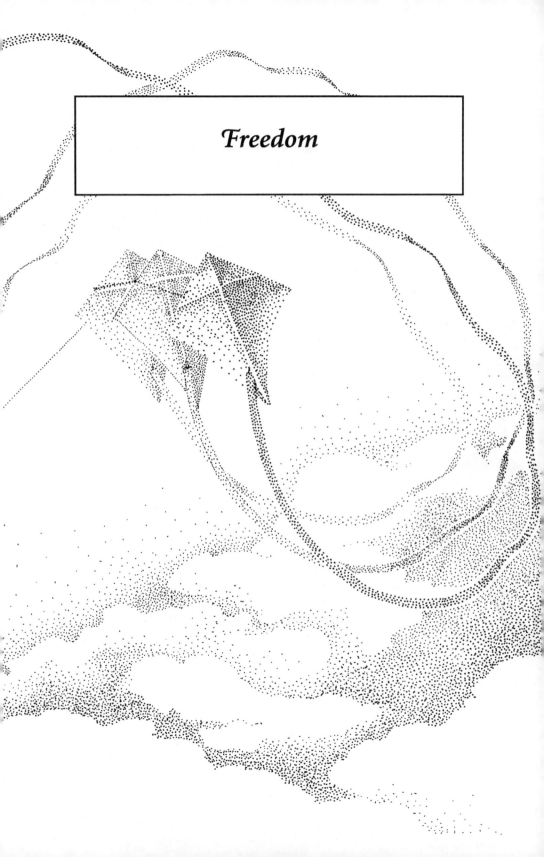

Freedom

Choose Life

Sometimes we are prisoners in prisons of our own design. We've carefully built our walls; we've made our prison safe and comfortable, and then we have chosen to lock ourselves inside. And we do not call it a prison at all, we call it our home or work or responsibility. We are very careful to post guards so that nothing threatens the security of our prison. Some of us live and die there and suppose that we have been happy and that living was good.

But sometimes, something or someone happens to us and the walls are shattered, and we lie helpless and exposed . . . in view are new horizons, new ideas, new experiences. When this happens many of us quickly gather the stones and rebuild our prison and retreat inside, but some few look around and crawl out of the rubble and gaze into the distance and wonder what "stuff" the world is made of. They venture out to taste and smell and feel. These people never build prisons again. They are willing to risk the hurt and possible failure of living and loving and dying with no guarantee of safety. They live with only the promise that there is fullness in living. They take the risk and choose life.

Molly Dee Rundle

Boxes

God, I want to be free.
Free—physically, spiritually, and emotionally.
I want to be free to feel and to experience.
No fences, no bounds, no limitations—no boxes.
I want to be me.
But, God, I'm not free.
Others have built fences around me.
And I have created boxes of doubt and frustration
in my own heart and mind.
God, take complete control of my life and
open all my neatly tied boxes.

Barbara Lee Brown

For Every Woman

For every woman who is tired of acting weak when she knows she is
    strong,
there is a man who is tired of appearing strong when he feels
    vulnerable.

For every woman who is tired of acting dumb,
there is a man who is burdened with the constant expectation of
    "knowing everything."

For every woman who is tired of being called "an emotional female,"
there is a man who is denied the right to weep and to be gentle.

For every woman who is called unfeminine when she competes,
there is a man for whom competition is the only way to prove his
    masculinity.

For every woman who is tired of being a sex object,
there is a man who must worry about his potency.

For every woman who feels "tied down" by her children,
there is a man who is denied the full pleasures of shared parenthood.

For every woman who is denied meaningful employment or equal pay,
there is a man who must bear full financial responsibility for another
    human being.

For every woman who was not taught the intricacies of an automobile,
there is a man who was not taught the satisfaction of cooking.

For every woman who takes a step toward her own liberation,
there is a man who finds the way to freedom has been made a little
    easier.

Nancy R. Smith

Chains

Whether by chains
or by beautiful ribbons
we are tied,
it makes no difference.
In fact,
in all probability,
it would be easier
to break the chains
because we associate ribbons
with beauty
and cannot see
that they are tied around us
to keep us
in our place.

Lydia Saenz

Pockets

Her given name was Emily,
But everyone called her "Pockets."
They called her that
because she insisted over and over again
that people shouldn't own anything
they can't carry
in their pockets.

For a while
Emily traveled light,
living her pocket philosophy to the letter.
However,
it didn't take long at all
to fill the four and a half pockets
in her jeans.

A resourceful person,
Emily became a regular customer
of the local Army Surplus stores.
She bought garments with abundant pockets
designed to carry K-Rations
                    Bullets
                    Maps

Snake-Bite Kits
P.X. Chocolate
Canteens
and
Assorted Survival Gear.

Emily soon filled these pockets
toward her own survival.

She carried Money
Canned Goods
Rye Bread
Instant Coffee
Panty Hose
Paperback Books
A Clarinet
24 Green and 7 yellow pills
13 Pairs of Earrings
2 Bottles of Apple Wine
and
An Electric Toothbrush (with
Manual Paste).

As time passed
Emily added more and more clothes
with more and more pockets
to hold more and more things.
She was indeed proud
that she had never compromised
and used even one shopping bag.

Emily was last seen
somewhere in Southern California
standing very, very still.
She was wearing (several layers of clothes
under) a woolen Army greatcoat
on which she had sewn large pockets
to hold
her folding bicycle
a television
and
a complete set of the Great Books of the
Western World.

Patricia M. Ryan

Litany

Leader: Who are you?

Response: I am woman.

Leader: What kind of woman are you?

Response: I am every woman.

Leader: But who are you?

First voice: I am a sheltered lady with a successful husband. He furnishes me with my every need and desire. I keep busy making myself beautiful. Don't try to change women's status. Women are happy as they are.

Second voice: I am a Third World woman. I have known discrimination of women all my life by my government, my culture, my heritage, and my family. I have no status. I work at hard labor the same as the men, yet I have borne and buried many babies. What is liberation? Will it free me from hunger and help my children? I need only to survive and keep my children alive! Will liberation do that?

Third voice: I am a professional woman with political and economic power. I have worked years to achieve, and here at the top there is room for only a few of us women. So don't change the status quo. I like it the way it is. Women do not need liberation, for we *are* liberated . . . at least enough of us are for now.

Fourth voice: I am a young woman whose days are crowded with children, husband, home, and family responsibilities; as well as church, school, and community activities. Some of my busy days I feel happy and glad. Other times I feel trapped and smothered with the monotony of years of meals, laundry, dishes, and clutter. I sometimes seek, but in vain, for time to express my own creativity. I need more time alone. Liberation? It seems so far away.

Fifth voice: I am a widow and a grandmother. My family is grown and gone. We visit each other once a year. The rest of the time I am alone. I'd like to be busy in a creative job, for I have my health and one-third of my life stretches out before me, but doors of opportunity close in my face. I have no special skills or training. My experience of being a housewife and a mother for over thirty years impresses no employers. I am not needed by anyone anymore. I need to be liberated from being alone and lonely.

Response: We are every woman—young, middle-aged, and old. We are all races, all classes. We are worldwide. We are every woman. We shall be liberated and we shall be free, but not until all of our sisters and all of our brothers are free. For none of us can find liberation until all of us have found it.

All: "There is neither Jew nor Greek, there is neither slave nor free,
there is neither male nor female; for you are all one in Christ Jesus."

Garnett Lee Bond

Frightening Freedom

Did you know that the early Christians were accused of cannibalism
by outsiders who misunderstood the Communion ritual? Non-
Christians were fearful and believed that the Christians actually ate
human flesh. The outsiders also assumed that the early Christians
were anarchists because they spoke of a different kind of kingdom.
What might these strange people with such new and radical ideas do if
left alone?

Of course, those outsiders were really the "insiders"—the people
who had the power in the non-Christian culture of those days. Thus
the early Christians suffered from misunderstanding—based partly on
a misunderstanding of symbolic words and actions and largely on the
fear within those who could not bear to have society shaken up and
changed by such new ideas.

Change *is* frightening! It is more comfortable to follow prescribed
roles and procedures, yet we all complain about them. Into this society
change is coming. We see new attitudes.

Clearly articulated is the belief that each person is unique, with the
right to choose his or her own future and to fulfill his or her own
God-given potential. People need the freedom and genuine opportunities for this task, without the protections and constraints of former
roles.

It is frightening to realize that our life can be really our own, that
we *have* the freedom to live as we choose, without depending on
others' expectations. We don't know how to use that kind of freedom
in our kind of world!

But the message of the Gospel is that God loves us! The Creator
made us and calls that creation good. With the gift of life comes the
gift of freedom to *live* that life.

Prayer: I accept my freedom, O God, even though I am fearful of
forging into new and unknown ways of living. I rejoice that the
Women's Movement challenges me to a new understanding of the
freedom you offer to all of us and the responsibility to be transformed
into a new person. Amen.

Nancy R. Smith

Primitive Eve

So long I've been shedding layers of my skin.
And now, deep from the surface, I stand naked.
Waiting, not hidden.
To be seen, to be touched.
Sentient cells quivering, airy aspects
Counting abstractions I left behind,
Tender new skin pink with fright.
I'm shocked to be nude.
Audacious moment, to stand bare, uncovered.
Here I stand visible, shorn, without guile.
Exposed.
But to what?
Will new layers come in exchange for those already sloughed off?
Repelled by that thought, I'm cold and need warmth.
Chilled from platitudes, I'm afraid of that comfort.
I have no secrets now, emptied of illusions.
So here I stand like a Primitive Eve before her fig leaf, barefoot,
    entranced with her act.
Here I am—still yet—the fact of myself.
Here, ready—waiting.

Adele Allen

A Litany of Awareness

One woman: This is a time to see where we are and where we are
    going. We have often felt alone.
All women: We have been taught to hold in contempt the members of
    our own sex. We know physical isolation from other women
    imposed on us by our culture. We read books on "How to Be a
    Woman" written by men.
One man: We have often felt alone.
All men: We have not always wanted to perform as providers in jobs
    that remove us for long hours from our families. We do not always
    feel like protectors.
One woman: We are trapped and alienated by language.
Everyone: We hear the words of psychiatry:
Reader: "That women must be regarded as having little sense of
    justice is no doubt related to the predominance of envy in their
    mental life."
Everyone: We hear the words of politics:

Reader: "The small influence of women in state leadership is in large measure due to women's own inertia."

Everyone: We hear the words of religion:

Reader: On admitting women to the priesthood: "I cannot see a single reason for discarding the logic and religious experience of thousands of years in order to gratify the longing a handful of women have for recognition and power."

One man: We feel trapped by stereotypes.

All men: When we have wanted to be gentle, we have been programmed to believe that gentleness is not masculine. When we have longed to weep, we are informed that weeping is for women. When we have admitted that we enjoy cooking and sewing, we are told that those are not suitable occupations for "real men."

One woman: We have known exploitation.

All women: We have worked at identical jobs for half the salary of men. We have learned to value wrinkleless skin over intellectual achievement. We have been made helpmates, temptresses, and dependents, as though our individuality meant nothing. The sanctity of a clean wash overrode our sanctity as persons.

One man: We have tasted the use of illegitimate power and found it bitter, because we see that we as well as our sisters suffer from this exploitation.

All men: Some of us have said, "No woman should take a job away from a man"—as if men were the sole providers for families. At the same time, we have invited our own dehumanization in our ruthless competition for more money and better jobs. We have found ourselves wishing for hostesses to wait on us and secretaries to serve us. We have seemed unaware that women are unique individuals, not servile creatures.

Everyone: But there have been voices calling us to awareness.

One: "I came not to the whole and the powerful, but to the weak."

Everyone: We listen joyfully to those voices.

One: "You are all one in Christ!"

Everyone: We are moving with the rhythms of those voices, moving. . . .

One: ". . . Beyond all known standards . . . beyond, to a species with a new name, that would not dare define itself as Man."

All women: It's a great time to be a woman!

All men: It's a great time to be a man!

Everyone: It's a great time to be a person!

Linda K. Beher

A Prayer for Justice

Holy Friend,

New freedoms have trickled into our lives so slowly that we've been almost unaware of them.

Now we revel in the joy of fresh waters. Yet we wade about in the shallows and think we are swimming!

When we dare to listen, we hear you say, "Launch out into the deep." But as we feel the rising stream, we are disturbed by changing concepts of justice for others as well as for ourselves.

We view our new freedoms gratefully, but inside them you've placed such heavy responsibilities. We hadn't quite counted on this, God! Yet, you made us and you made the depths, and these are the days of our years.

Overflow our hearts with the healing of liberation. May loving justice flood our dreams for those still enslaved. Never let us rest until our emancipation is shared with all those persons who are dispossessed or alienated.

We pray in the name of Jesus who went about doing good.
Amen.

Hazel Nowell Ailor

One to One

Two Trees

A portion of your soul has been
    entwined with mine.
A gentle kind of togetherness, while
    separately we stand.
As two trees deeply rooted in
    separate plots of ground,
While their topmost branches
    come together,
Forming a miracle of lace
    against the heavens.

Janet Miles

He Won't Listen

I am alone. I have been alone for weeks now. It pains me. I hurt so deep. Each day brings a newer and larger dimension of loneliness. The person who "should" be with me is away, has been for months, even though we live together daily. I have tried and tried to communicate. The line must have shut down completely for I am not allowed to say my thoughts anymore.

I am alone. My disappointment tonight is real and will loom large in my mind for weeks, I think.

No one to appreciate me tonight. I felt pretty—almost beautiful—and happy. At this moment only tears and hurt.

I am alone.

Nobody must know. I don't even think anybody cares. I am fairly sure he won't care to hear me tonight.

"How was your party," he'll ask. I'll answer, knowing he really doesn't care, "Oh, it was fun." But he won't listen anymore. After all he wasn't there, and I think he won't hear even that small exchange.

Our worlds have turned into tight little balls. Neither of us is open with one another anymore. I think that I have tried, but time and time again we end in fights and more fights.

I am alone. O God, I can never be alive and open again with these lonely thoughts. I am alone night after night. How much longer can I go on being alone?

And now I'll go take off my pretty new dress. After all, Cinderella had to return to the chimney and soot, didn't she? Only she had a happy ending. I think there are no princes around anymore.

Name withheld

Planting Vineyards

If you would be friend to me
    don't say "I love you."
    Don't call me special or unique.
Just take the time to know me.

I need your love
    and affirmation too much
    to clutch at the straw of words.

How easily words flow
    in this new Christianity!
Everyone loves everyone.

The whole world
    is the whole world's lover!

But I am not the whole world.
    I am me.
And I don't know
    who I am anymore.
If I ever did.

I don't want your promiscuous loving.
Give that to the faceless world.
But could we take the time
    to be friends?
Is there time for that
    in this era of instant caring?

Do you have the time
    before rushing on to the next conquest?

It must be terribly important
    to save the world
if we can't stop to plant vineyards.

Donna Swanson

~

How many am I?
With all my children's children
Love makes me plural.

Jean Fox Holland

Release Your Captives

For twelve years I drank my coffee black and complained loudly over the necessity of setting out cream and sugar for my husband every meal. Then, while visiting relatives, I decided I preferred my coffee with cream. For weeks back home I struggled with pride, wanting to put cream in my coffee but fearing my husband's reaction. At last one morning I asked for the cream. He looked at me with surprise and asked simply, "How long have you been using cream?" and passed it to me. Joy! He had let me change. I was no longer trapped by my past behavior.

How hard it is to let other people change and grow! We box them in with our picture of them. We think, "He wouldn't want to do that. She's never done this before. They aren't interested in that sort of thing."

Jesus allowed people to change. He expected great things of them. He let them respond as free individuals. Do we?

Joyce Flight

How Smart Are You?

Fold your wisdom in a locket,
little woman. Close the lid
and let it dangle like a jewel
on a silver chain.

Hide your wisdom in your pocket,
pretty woman. Keep it hid.
I do not want to feel
you challenging me again.

Make your sweet mouth shyly silent;
let me be the stronger one
with the gifts of thought and speech
in my command.

You are woman, you are golden
as the mute and fiery sun.
Drop your wisdom in the gutter,
pretty woman, take my hand.

Greta Schumm

New Horizons

You're a woman now, my daughter,
I can see it in your eyes
Feel it in your enthusiasm.
Your world is no longer
bounded by ours.
It stretches out
to new horizons
with pathways
of your choosing.
Go quickly now
else I'm too tempted
to call you back
to continue the interweaving
of twenty beautiful years.
But
when you're free
come back—
come back as my friend
so that
our worlds can meet
at the intersection
of love
and respect.

Jean Spencer

A Gift

you have touched me
you have cradled me in your security
until i found my own
given me words
when they were unknown to me
tenderly you have held my heart in your hands
your firmness has given me strength
life itself wrapped in love
was your first gift to me
to love you is to love myself
to love myself is to love you

Mary Eleanore Rice

Empathy in Sheer Places

There was enough fear for a mountain,
so we scaled it in words, inch by inch.
You and I, yoked by a fragile rope,
climbing a steep conversation,
way past footholds, we were slipping, dangling
over everything vulnerable within us.
(You wore me like a pendant, heavily,
while your shadow moved on my face
like a perishable wonder.)
A cloud pressed us against fossil places in the rock
until we were marked—tattooed—
with truths about each other
that no one had ever cared
to take upon themselves.
Immobile in the wind,
we were braced against the crag
with only the rope while invisibly, geometrically
through conversation being spun, a web
from me toward you, from you toward me
would risk the love that saved us.

Marilyn MacCanon Brown

My Firstborn's Gone to College

All those days
   And all those years
         Stretch out in an expanse
   So endless I am drowned almost
Breathless, choking, gasping from the effort
   Of all the reaching, remembering, reaching
   And all that living, loving, living.

In a vertigo of shifting, change, and borning
         I am still.
Looking back,
   Releasing the past unto itself,
      Recalling in order to let go. . . .

Mary Frances Palmer

A Circle

In
the
pause
of prayer
I
think of
persons
brought closer
to me.

In
the
midst
of persons,
I think
of
prayer,
setting them
free.

Anita Wheatcroft

Affirmation of Faith

Women of faith, who before I was born, had conceived how faith and freedom are one with God's purpose. They, my foresisters, lived and died that my faith and life could have more freedoms. Because of them, I can answer God's call. Because of them, I take strength from the past to continue their work to change the future. Women of yesterday and women of today all conceive that someday we will all be one, equal in love, in responsibility, and in power in the world and in the church. Women of faith, women of the past, you are present in my faith and in my future. You are here, present in the struggle for the birth of the future.

Chris Blackburn

Hills to Climb

Have you ever climbed
    a high high hill
Hoping all the while
    to find some beauty dust
    on the other side?

Have you ever loved someone
    who could not return your love,
But yet, you hoped and
    climbed your own
    private hills
And found only valleys
    on the other side
    instead of love?

Have you ever reached the summit of ecstasy
    only to find in its place
Awaited tears and astonishment
    at your own naivete in believing
    and hoping and dreaming?

Yet, you and I cannot have touched
    or loved or cried together
Without each of us changing a little . . .
For you will never be the same,
I will never be the same,
And our lives will never be the same. . . .

I shall remember, after a while,
After the hurt is gone,
Only the good times,
The fun times,
The love times,
Only the best in you . . .
Which was what I wanted to see
Exclusively,
Anyway. . . .

Sharon West Lansing

Unique

"I" is such a slender word,
   a selfish word.
"We" is broader and enchanting
   for it doubles the outlook.

Mary Paquette

To My Love, and Mostly to Myself

I am not a bottle of Jergens lotion
   poured out on the world's pain,
I am not the alter ego of husband,
   sons, daughters.

I love you and that tells me something
   important about both of us.
But it does not tell me who I am.
Before we were together, I was,
   by myself.
If I were to lose you, I would grieve
   and feel desolation, but I would prevail.
That I can join with you is an
   incredible richness to me.
It is cause for singing and dancing
   and being glad.
But it is I who sing my song and
   you who sing yours.
I do not become you. I am myself.
I may dance with you, but I am
   not you. I am myself.
You can only help me and I, you,
   if we are apart from one another,
Two of us, reciprocal.

Martha Whitmore Hickman

To My Daughter, Great with Child

She seemed withdrawn tonight.
We were always close
And the baby
Draws us closer.
Yet tonight,
I thought she seemed
Tuned in to another frequency.
Is it just
That I'm so old?
So far removed?
Oh, I know she doesn't think
I'm really ancient,
But to her
It's been so long
Since I, too, went through
The joys and fears
Of gazing at my own distended flesh.
It's been a lifetime—
Her very lifetime—
And that must seem long ago!
Could it be
That she's retreating?
Retreating from the periphery
Of normal living?
Withdrawing from the trivia
In order to hone in
On the realities?
To focus on the only relevant
For this time?
She's strewing farewell notes
To herself as she was,
And picking up clues
For herself as she will be.
She seems
To be garnering her forces,
Gathering herself together
In tighter and tighter circles,
In close concentric circles,
Refining her strengths
Strengthening her resolves,
Draining off the dross
Of all busy involvement,

In order to come complete
To her confinement.
A novice who does homage
To the order,
She sits in quiet meditation.
She responds to
Rigid inner disciplines,
And never ceases her ablutions,
Never ceases preparation
For the Advent,
Ever holy.
She hardly knows I'm here,
So I tiptoe, quiet, away,
Smiling all the while
As I see her reverent face,
And see her
Genuflect
To
Life!

Normagene Warner

Love

Love is acceptance
   no matter what the color
      long the hair
      new the car
      dull the remark
      bad the kids
      old the dress
      loud the voice
      foreign the thought.

Love is listening
      hearing
      learning
      caring
      feeling
      sharing . . .
         . . . loving.

Mary Ellen Jesson

The Image of God

Man
here I am
a woman.

Let me take your hands
both hands in mine
and ask that you would look at me
straight—eye to eye.

Accept me as I am
Honor my integrity.
Love me as an equal child of God
made with you
in God's own image.

Frances Marian Lightbourn

For Chistians, Parting

So, in the end, we leave;
we do not say good-by.

Lot's wife may turn;
Dido, disconsolate try

To keep the past a now.
But you and I

(And all who live
and love in Christ) must know

I do not wholly stay
you do not truly go. . . .

"In Christ there is no East or West,"
We sing—
and *live?* This is the test
Beloved, this is the test.

Amen.

Sr. Mary Catherine Vukmanic, OSU

A Love Poem

Know
That two human beings
Have shared
And share.

Know
That two
Have lessened
The walls between
One human being
And another;
Because of this,
There be lesser walls with others.

Know
That care and concern
Cost so little
When we open our eyes
To the world.

But also know
That care and concern
Cost much:
Commitment and striving.

Know
That because of this knowledge
One forgives others
And remembers
The strength
We have and share.

Know
That because we share
The world is changed
And we are changed
Forever.

Know.

Nancy D. Wayne

If Anyone Waves Toward Me I Wave Back
(*On seeing, from the train window, some boys waving as we go past*)

Since by no laser beam of revelation
We are known to one another,
Since the whole urge of life seems to know and make known
The edges of the inexpressible Secret,
Since arm will still and glass darken
And no fragment can or should be squandered,
Since the boys out the window, quickly, in fact and principle, recede—
If anyone waves toward me I wave back.

Since I, now going back to husband, children,
Have left my father's house for the fortieth time, and my childhood,
    again,
Since his near-death from illness
Tells us what we all know: a time will come when he will not recover,
Since my heart breaks with the love I would tell him if I could
But I am, so my life decrees, stable, adult, middle-aged, and I do not
    with every word, cry,

And since home, left, gone back to, will not be renamed in any terms
    but its own—
If anyone waves toward me I wave back.

Since those boys who wave from the mound of gray snow as the train
    goes by
Will one day be within and I without, above or below the ground,
Since my wish for them is that they wave as long as they can
Before some middle decorum between innocence and innocence
    constrains them,
Since what I wave to is the boys, is my father, is myself,
Is the Secret in its every rendition in youth or in age or in tree or in
    person,
Since (though they probably do not see me) there is a thousand-to-
    one chance they might see me watching and I wouldn't be waving—
If anyone waves toward me I wave back.

Martha Whitmore Hickman

Pain and Sorrow

Gift

Grant me the gift of telling you my grief.
I shall not voice it often, for I know
Entrenchment of the widely held belief
That bravery requires scars must not show.
But if you are my friend, please understand
My need to tell you of this devastation.
I will learn silence, but your ear and hand
Just now could start a healing consolation.

Hazel Nowell Ailor

A Litany for a Somber Morning

There is rain. Voices from the hill filter down through a soft weeping.

TAKE AWAY MY PAIN, GOD. TAKE AWAY MY GRIEF.

The rain is soft and clean, and washes away a face to wear for crowds
that do not care.

CLEANSE ME, GOD. SHOW ME THE CHILD I ONCE WAS.

Footprints that marked the easy path up the orchard are melted into
mud.

BATHE MY FEET, GOD, PLEASE. TAKE THE WORLD AWAY.

Fruit that fell from the trees is bruised and crushed.

FORGIVE ME, GOD. I LET IT WASTE.

Find the tree at the top of the hill. Pick the ripe fruit. Wash it in the
rain. Savor its sweet juice.

THANK YOU, GOD. IT IS GOOD. AND YOU HAVE BID ME COME, CLEAN AT
LAST, AND WHOLE, TO BE FILLED WITH THE FRUIT.

Now there is sun, and a breeze, and much to do.

AMEN.

Elinor J. George

Endings

over . . . finished
ready to start again
endings are only a necessity
a necessity for new beginnings
new beginnings can be nurtured forever

Mary Eleanore Rice

My Rock Wall

Long has my rock wall towered
above the trees in this place.
Today, unexpectedly,
my rock wall blooms.
Sheer granite sports flowers amid the quartz;
foliage atop the feldspar.
How can this be?

Long have winds and sands blown harsh
against my rock.
Attrition (as sorrow)
has etched most deeply
into my rock face.
And in good time,
God has filled those crevices
with seeds and soil.
I, unknowing,
have thought myself a rock
a habitat of eagles and lichens.
Behold, I am also a garden!

True, flowers (as joy) wither away.
Sorrow's crevices reappear;
The eagles and lichens alone will remain.
But had there been no harsh winds
would my rock wall have bloomed?
Had there been no sorrow,
would I know such joy?

Linda Felver

Of Words and Wine

O God,
Say words over my wineskins
    Water become wine
    Salt, sweet

I bear salt water in wineskins
that may burst from the burden
       futile yesterdays
       nights that mist around the now
       trackless tomorrows

Say words over my wineskins
    Water become wine
    Salt, sweet
Death become living love.

Elinor J. George

~

One who knows sorrow
For a long or little while
Learns a new language.

Jean Fox Holland

It's Too Early to Quit

It's always too early to quit.
Edison proved that in his laboratory.
Earth, being dug, often reveals a seed ready to sprout.
Hasty ending to aborted beginning.
In a survival of the fittest, love is strong.
Sometimes it needs a fallow period,
To gain strength, to become richer,
To rest, not quit, not be forgotten.
Love needs to be thought,
To be evaluated, and then a sorting out, a separation of parts.
The pruned tree often looks dead but the life is not in the appearance,
But in the hidden spark that didn't quit.

Adele Allen

The Scalded Dog

As a scalded dog
Avoids the kitchen,
Dodging the cook
And the swinging door,
So I flee the refuge
Of my sanctuary,
Finding no comfort
In the familiar clichés,
The comfortable pews,
The pious genuflecting
Of my former self.

But the wild dog
Is a lean dog,
A hungry dog,
A lonesome, broken dog
Who still must live
On the crumbs from some table.
So it furtively haunts
The trash barrels of its neighborhood,
The refuse heaps of its city.

And I?
I am sifting, sifting—
Clawing through the debris
Of my broken shattered faith,
Searching for crumbs.
Crumbs crucial for my very existence!

Normagene Warner

Open to the Storm

We cannot abandon life because of its storms. The strongest trees are not found sheltered in the safety of the forest, rather they are out in the open spaces—bent and twisted by winds of all seasons. God provides deep roots when there are wide-spreading branches.

Tammy Felton

Hiatus

This weather matches my mood.
Turbulent—
Thunder gathering—
Rolling—muffled crash!
Clouds boiling
torn off wisps
whipping by
like dirty veils.
Heat so close,
so heavy
I can't breathe.
Lightning skipping
on and off
or blinding flash
cuts a ragged streak
across the sky!

Momentary flashes of insight.
Oppressive knowledge that it's done.
No change for what is past—
bad or good.
Fighting hesitation—
"Will I err again?"
Best sit here like a stone,
blind and dull and heavy;
no longer hurt
nor giving hurt.

A sudden gust
of cool, fresh wind!
Awareness
that the gentle rain
is soaking into
thirsty earth
and all the
growing things
are dancing
in the breeze
and washing clean!

Surprise awareness
of a tear
seeping from a source
long parched and dry

washed bare by floods of grief
long past and gone.
Has Time, the gentle healer,
done its work
and made a place
for hope to grow?

Sophia E. Smith

Dear God,

My props are out from under me today,
    maybe they were the wrong kind of props.
Fear is creeping through the cracks
    like little insects of prey.
My aloneness gathers around my shoulders.
    I long for the feel of loving arms instead.

But thank you, God,
    for the real knowing that under all of these feelings
    your everlasting arms are around me.
Help me now to lean back and feel that security.
I push and pull and struggle
    to live life as I think I should.
But maybe I strive for vain expectations
    in ways I am not fully aware.

Calm and quiet my soul that there may be no
    inward fight between my ambitions and my limitations.
But, O God, don't ever let self-concern
    for these physical disturbances take over
    and become so important that I lose sight of you
And my own contribution to life as you meant it to be.

Thank you for not giving your children
    the spirit of fear, but of power
    and of love, and of a sound mind.
With power, love, and a sound mind
    help me to be free from fear.
I can move forward with joy
    even through the dark moments that come.

Thank you, God.

Pauline Reeder Liddle

Detachment

The name of the gift shop in the East Pavilion of Barnes Hospital is "The Wishing Well." In this highly sensitized state I'm living in, where I see symbolism in every word or phrase, this in itself is a wry misnomer. When the kindly ladies from The Wishing Well ask, "May I help you?" I must always repress the jarring reply, "Yes, I've come to have my son made well, if you please, Ma'am" and say instead, "Is this sixty-nine-cent jar the only size you have?" This week The Wishing Well is featuring a pair of cuddly teddy bears locked in close embrace—the red one is hugging the white one. How delightfully cunning, how endearing, until one sees the startling tag "To detach simply unsnap the fasteners." Then I see that the simulated affection is caused by gripper snaps strategically placed in paws and body fur. "Unsnap to detach."

I know the medical staff must have a certain area of detachment in order to efficiently do its work. I haven't wanted anyone operating on Steve with tear-dimmed eyes, but how glad I am for the ones who still risk the ache that inevitably comes with identifying with our dying son Stephen. There are a few nurses who have held me as I wept, and a few whose tears have mingled with mine. They somehow give me a little hope in this whole unreal, cockeyed, hopeless experience. There is a bond that holds us together as human beings—there is a standard—someone cares. It is frightfully important to me that human beings still weep and rage at injustice and unfairness. Some of the nurses and the doctors have successfully built a wall around the deep place of the heart so they are not vulnerable to the agonies they see. They have detached the gripper snaps. They have forgotten what a hand on the shoulder reached out in pity and remorse can mean—*nor can they know until they subject themselves to vulnerability and pain by the risk of identity.*

What are the bonds of love? The glad affirmation that reassures me now is that they are as natural as the next breath and as constant as a heartbeat! Not to have wondered about them but just to have had them and accepted them is a testament to the depth and reality of those bonds.

And now I find that death itself cannot break those bonds of love. Detachment? Impossible! I could no more detach myself from Steve than I could remove my heart from my breast. Some persons find comfort in the euphemism *lost* as a substitute for the harsher *died.* Now I'm surer than ever that lost is inappropriate. *Lose* Stephen? Never! He is inextricably bound in the heart of each of us and will flow through us, enriching us forever. The little teddy bears are literally cute, but how meaningless is an embrace that depends on gripper snaps? Bone of my bone and flesh of my flesh, I am bound by the invasive fibers of love and these are undetachable.

Normagene Warner

It Would Be Easier

It would be easier
If things were absolute;
Not like human beings,
Unsure, unpredictable,
    Forever many-sided.

But, then, living and becoming
Are not easy
And we would not grow
Or come to You
If it were.

Nancy D. Wayne

Death

Death, I am afraid of you.
You covet what is mine and take from me
    without my being able to hold on . . .
                        push back . . .
                            protect.
I do not want to know you.
Your counterparts are risk and chance
    and missing guarantees.
To be at ease with you removes a wall
                    behind which I can hide
                    and feel secure when
                    all else fails.
Yet, I am being pushed and nudged into
    new realms of comprehension.
It is the Christ who points the way.
His life is death, and death is life—
    all bound in one creative whole.
I hear the Word: "Be not afraid of death, without denying life."
I need your strength, my God,
    to help me understand and know
    that giving is receiving, and letting go is having all.

Alma Roberts

A Prayer for the Dying

She is dying, God.
It surrounds her like a halo.
In the afternoon, in the heat, we talk.
We talk of living while she dies.
The disease has painted her eyes black.
Her skin has turned yellow and her stomach is swollen.

Swollen she is, God. Like a woman with life inside
But God, God, God, her womb carries death.
Her lipstick smile is grotesque in the heat of the afternoon.
Her eyes are large in wonder and awe.
And we talk of the trivia of the unhurried living,
While she dies.

Paint by number, paint by number, paint by number
Red, green, yellow, blue, fill in the lines, fill them in.
While she empties out. In July while the sweat trickles down.
And we play the game together. Pretend you are blind.

She is dying, God.
She forgets to mention it in the conversation.
But she says it with a frightened soul that speaks to mine.
And while our tongues speak of weather or church or children.
Our souls exchange bitter tears. Because that is all to do.

And a few months. Perhaps a year. How many days?
Her son, husband, sisters, or mother. One of them will call.
It will be over. They will ask me to bury her.
Bury her in words they'll want. And in the ground.
And I will. It is my job.

But, God, when no one sees, while they mourn beyond reality,
I will reach into me and give this of mine to her.
And we will be buried together along with the silence of now.
In the snow, or the spring, or perhaps in the heat of an afternoon.
When we no longer pretend. When the talk is the tears.

Sharon M. Freeto

The Needs of Others

Word of God

Gesticulating violently
arms flail in air.
Fragments of exhortations
float about the room
and, finding no response,
settle vaguely
like dust
on the furniture.
"Bring the names of your unsaved loved ones to the altar."

My patients sit unheeding,
wheelchairs lining the walls
like canned goods on grocery shelves,
each in its own compartment.
The Word of God spills loudly into the room.
"God loves you," carol the singers brightly.
"Whatever keeps you from the House of God on the Lord's Day is a
    sin," thunders the preacher.
Faces are immobile, vacant, and (I hope) uncomprehending.
Is old age a sin, man of God?

Bawl and rage about the sins of society;
your glib words clutter this room
already so overladen with suffering, loneliness,
desolation, despair, and death.
Your wordy Word increases the burden.
Lay aside your words.
Cease babbling promises.
Moisten the lips of a dying woman.
Learn to trim toenails with respect
in awareness of that person's dignity as a human being.
Suffer.
Kneel.
Sit face-to-face with degenerative disease.
The Word of God is wordless here.

Linda Felver

The Communion

Blind and alone she sat on her bed
and sang
an old hymn
from an old church.

She sang for herself.

Her sound came from somewhere
deep in her being,
to sing was her need.

Her needing made me stop.

And somewhere between her singing
and my stopping
something happened
that had never happened to me before.

I entered her room.

I said in faulted Spanish:
I come with God
with Jesucristo
for you.

And she shook into tears.

I come with the Holy Communion
El Cuerpo
de Jesucristo
por tu.

She began to nod
and her blind, closed eyes wept.

Somehow her desire had reached
me and the surprise and joy
could not be contained in
words or smiles.

And she said: I was so alone.

And I said: Jesucristo has come;
I have come;
and I held her
and tried to talk
but we were beyond words.

Catharine Stewart Roache

Synchronized Hearts

World travelers have been made aware when traveling through various time zones, of the impossibility of synchronizing clocks, marking time for the peoples of the world. The youthful idea that we Americans are superior at everything, especially building a high quality standard of living, must be put aside while the truth is laid bare.

We must finally come to grips with the fact that peoples whom we hope to remold, to fit into our mental picture of what they should be, cannot ever be forced into our time pattern. Not only have some completed the day we are just beginning, but if we stop to really investigate, we might find they are way ahead of us in many other aspects of life. The most important thing to synchronize is our hearts, where compassion is born, letting it out so that others may come to depend on it. A simple life is easy to lead when one knows someone cares.

Edna C. Neureuther

A Mother Is a Person

a mother is a person
who gives birth
cleans up messes
kisses dirty faces
makes thousands of peanut butter sandwiches
and says no more often than yes

a mother is a person
who acts as chauffeur
personal secretary
and general contractor
housebreaks and feeds the dog
hunts for numerous lost articles
and hurts when her child is hurt

a mother is a person
who needs to remember
she is a person

Mary Eleanore Rice

One Dream on Rye to Go

Lucille was very difficult to talk to.
You see,
she lived inside a dream
and no one else
was allowed in.

In the early days
Lucille would come out for supper.
But that stopped as soon as she discovered
that the local delicatessen
would deliver.

At first
Lucille's dream
was just a comfortable, marshmallow buffer
between herself
and the rest of the world.

But the dream grew
a little every day.
It thickened like pudding
and began to float further and further off the ground.
Soon there was no reaching Lucille.
Even the man with the pickles and pastrami
couldn't get in.

Lucille's family and friends
tied heavy ropes around the dream
and took turns holding her down.
They struggled valiantly
with the ropes.
But the dream continued to grow
until finally
Lucille reached out
cut the ropes
and floated away.

Pat Ryan

Understanding

All of a sudden, God, it seems like everyone has discovered the word
    communication—
Youth and aged—both trying desperately to be understood.
Everyone hears but—is anyone out there listening?
What about those crying out in the night?
Is anybody listening to them?
God, do those who commit suicide cry out, too?
Teach us to use our minds with our ears.
Help us listen for that cry in the night!
And yet, "Grant that I may not so much seek to be understood, as to
    understand."

Barbara Lee Brown

For the Glory of God

Each of us gifted
with the alabaster jar,
we watch and listen for the time
when it is right to break it open,
spilling the precious insides
over what we have discovered
is eternal, good, and true.

There'll be noise about it.
"Not practical!"
"What a waste!"
"We didn't say you could do that!"
"You're wrong!"

But one voice,
whispering, maybe,
enters the chaos
and says for those who hear,

"Let her alone.
Why do you trouble her?
She has done
a beautiful thing for me."

Greta Schumm

Intercession for My Sisters

God, I am sustained by the living water you offer. Let me respond by helping those of my rural sisters whose chore of providing drinking water for their family proves a heavy burden. Forgive my former indifference to these needs. Thank you for the clean water that flows from my faucet. Thank you for the living waters you give so freely. Enable me to serve and share generously your gifts in ways that will make available to my sisters around the world the waters that liberate them to become more fully human. God, you always affirm our worth. You gave dignity to all women by your treatment. I seek to be your hands as I strive to ease the burdens of my rural sisters. *Amen.*

Carolyn Shinn

Involvement

Involvement!
God, I tremble when I hear the word.
How can I answer others' questions
When I can't answer my own?
How can I help them when I need help, too?
If I wait until I have all the answers,
I'll die—still waiting.
I'm afraid to try—but I'm more afraid of failing.
Help me, Holy Friend, to know my limitations;
And help me live with them.

Barbara Lee Brown

Reverberation

It was easy to bomb a church in Birmingham.
Few saw the faces there—
A black blur of little girls
Who laughed and sang,
Who cried in disbelief—
And then were silent . . .
So very silent that their weeping sounds
Above all the other sounds,
And I cannot rest for the clamor of their silence.

Hazel Nowell Ailor

To Be a Woman

To be a woman is to be alive as a creative person of God.

The ocean curls up on the shore, licking the sand until it is wet and waiting for me to scoop out a round area large enough to make a sand candle. On a small hibachi I melt the blue wax that matches the sky, wax collected from odd bits of candles, and pour it slowly into the receptive sand. I watch as it begins to harden into ripples of firmness and carefully insert a wick, holding it in place until I am sure it can stand alone. I create a candle.

I think about being a woman as I wait for my candle to become an independent creation, ready to glow and remind me of the majestic ocean and all of God's world.

To be a woman may mean to create a warm, living embryo within the body that will become a part of the world as a pulsating new creation. To many women this is an integral part of their being. I could not create a new life in this way, but one of my expressions of creation takes the form of helping to shape the lives of three adopted children. I look at them as they grow and mature and smile at their own unique possibilities. I say, "This is to be a woman, molding and shaping a human being, developing the potential of the fullness of God's creation, even as a sand candle is formed."

To be a woman means to me to be a loving, communicating wife, sharing in the responsibilities, problems, joys, and sorrows of daily living. It means together as husband and wife, living as one and yet independently and separately. We see our myriad cares as an essential part of life, even as the tiny grains of sand surround the blue wax of the candle.

To be a woman means, to me, to help not only at the beginning of life, but also at its ending. I see my sister slowly die from terminal cancer, I see a woman die with a failing heart, I see people in the hospitals and in homes coping with the process of dying, and behold the needs and cares of these persons. I see those who need a support- ive relationship as they struggle to cope with pain in the process of regaining health. Thus, even though I am prepared as a teacher, I then enter a career of nursing. I find this a meaningful possibility, holding these lives as the sand holds the wax until they are strong in life on earth or strong in their eternal life.

In the psychiatric wards of Saint Elizabeth's Hospital in Washington, D.C., I see many needs—the patient standing forlornly in the doorway looking for someone, the staring and vacant eyes of lonely souls, the alcoholics trying to cope with their problems, the results of drug abuse in young people, all symbolic of those who need help. I recog- nize this need for a loving, nonjudgmental relationship in an "I-thou" context. To me, to live creatively as a woman is to help bring these persons out of their shell-like existence, out of their hole, as it were, as I took the sand candle from its hollowed, curved sheltered spot.

Now my psychiatric training helps me in counseling at the Washington Pastoral Counseling Center to see a woman with tears needing to spill out her feelings of grief and hurt; to see a teenager gain confidence and independence as she copes with her problems; to see a couple learn to communicate with each other about their marriage; to see a woman work through her rejection by someone she loved; to recognize physical symptoms as they affect mental problems. My life finds expression in listening attentively and helping people deal with life.

To be a woman is to love creatively in many ways. I do not believe every woman lives in the same way, nor should she. For a woman has many potentialities and must find her own way of expression. There are unlimited possibilities for each woman to determine.

I create a sand candle. I strive to live each day with God so that I can be sensitive to the needs of others and respond with love. I light the sand candle. It glows. I feel God's presence within my life, giving the light that inspires me to thus live creatively.

Mary Ritzman Ebinger

Feed My Lambs

Night after night I see the starving baby
Hold her near, try to feed her milk.
I know our destinies are meshed, hers and mine.
Is it too late? Can she still be saved?
I join all sorrowing mothers in my dreams.

Week after week I see the Shepherd
At the altar where I bring my self—
Telling me to "feed my sheep and lambs."
Do I love enough to listen and obey?
Awake, I know I have some gifts to share.
I'm listening, Loving One, for you to tell me how.

Lura Houck Carstens

As Children Hurt

eyes
old tired eyes cover me and speak more
than words in any tongue can say
of what it is to hurt

hurt
as a child hurts
over little things
but what is little when you are old?

when you spend your days
lying, sitting, thinking, waiting
is it a little thing for someone to speak
without a hint of care?

when you live in one bed
in one room with one chest, one glass for six years
is it a little thing to be moved
without a word for the why?

when friends are far
and sick and moving and you fear they will forget
is it a little thing for one to die
and leave you more alone?

when night comes
and dark will give you peace and rest and quiet
is it a little thing to hear someone weeping
far down some hollow hall?

when you lie in hate
and despair of life, remembering good times, bad times
is it a little thing for your mouth to dry
into a yellow crust?

the world
tells me war is big
and profits and space and the price of gold
and I think about those things

but today
the cup of water seemed the world
and all those little things became
the only big.

Catharine Stewart Roache

The Rhythms of Life

Keep Me Whistlin'

I've heard the first call of the robins
For more than eighty years.
   And yet, today,
     hearing them once again,
     makes me want to sing.
(Can't sing!)

I've watched for countless springs
Graceful young things
   bounding on dancing feet,
   and seeing them today
   makes me want to leap and play.
(Can't leap—arthritis!)

It's long ago since I heard
A whippoorwill
   whistlin' away in the wood,
   but I heard one today—
   makes we want to
   whistle and play.
(Can't whistle—dentures!)

Yes, my throat is tight,
And my knees are stiff,
And my dentures rattle around a bit.
But in my heart, oh how I can sing.
How my spirit leaps,
How I laugh and spring!

God, keep me whistlin' merry tunes
Remembering lovely distant Junes,
Remembering birds
And flowers and fields
From the treasured harvest
Memory yields.

Sue C. Boynton

In Tune

Gracious God, I need you more
now that I am growing older.

Help me do less talking
and more listening,
less complaining
and more exclaiming.
Please, no bossing now,
just watching over
and standing by,
but not telling how.

Keep me from moodiness
and self-pity;
from repetitious words
set me free.
Keep me in tune
with the young,
Let me be carefree
enough to have fun.

Let me not think the world
has changed so much
that I grow bitter
and out of touch.
Let me use my experience
in much living
as an incentive
for more giving.

Gracious God, I need you much more now.

Charlotte Carpenter

~

Discovering that
Time's irrelevant at times
Is revelation.

Jean Fox Holland

Beauty

The rose is dead
My daughter said,
But see it gets
More beautiful.
How could a dead rose
Be beautiful in
Her little girl's eyes?
Is it because she dreams
Of new roses springing
From the stem of what
Seems to be gone?
New life from the
Death of the old.
She looks at dead things
Knowingly, her six-year-old
Faith is sure . . .
If mommy has new life
When her old one is gone,
Then surely new beauty
Will also grow when old
Beauty has flown.

Shirley M. Rogers

Limbo

some days i feel i need my life held
held in a holding pattern
held in limbo until
until i can proceed on my way
the need to stop and look
look back——and forward
not ready to proceed——just look
there seems to be a need to know
where i am now and
consider where i might go
some days are like that

Mary Eleanore Rice

For My Mother, Who Is Old

The sentences break off midway.
The glance looking to the window appears to stop at the pane, seeing
    nothing.
Or do you see something we do not?
What is it—can you tell me what that private vision is?
Is it old? Are you young again?
Am I?
Is he still here? your mother, father, too?

The words begin again and stop.
"That's why I don't have much to say," you say to me—
"I haven't the brain for it." A matter-of-fact impatience, tinged with
    wistfulness.
I demur, "It's late in the day," I say.
But how I miss you, Mother, in this moment, as I long to tell myself
    to you and you cannot hear it.
Then let us be together only, and I shall be my presence and you,
    yours,
While lilac bushes, bare in the winter wind,
Nod outside in the bleak air, brush against the glass
And stir against the window of your dreams.

Martha Whitmore Hickman

Fragments

    People
    pull pieces of me
    into their love and
    magnify those fragments
    into distortions of what
    I am.

    In my aloneness
    I dance and shout
    in the ever-expanding
    God-created wholeness of
    Me!

Marla Visser

The Ocean

I go to the ocean often
  To feel the sand move between my toes
  To sit quietly and become one with the ebb and flow of the tide.

I go to the ocean often
  To sense part of the eternal
  To experience a pulsing, growing beat within me, too, as a woman
    in this place, at this time.

I go to the ocean often
  To discover the moods of myself changing
  To reach out to the vast experience of the endless sea within.

I return home from the ocean slowly
  Climbing the dunes of sand and time
  Aware of the constant listening Mother Sea.

    Momentarily, I feel rocked, curved, cradled in her arms
    As fragile as a seashell
    Yes, as beautiful!

Marilyn Ray

Perhaps I'm Not Half-Bad After All

I have a friend who is beautiful,
But sees herself through flawed glass.
Her fine free humor comes out brash to her,
Foot in mouth.
Her perky features are her bane.
And yet, she finds me lovely
And makes a fuss when I
Keep looking in that
Self-same mirror.

What means it? When I see myself
So fat and homely, clumsy and cross,
She always finds me fair.
When I find her comely,
Her mirrors an ugly crone declare?

Shirley M. Rogers

Teach Me to Be Quiet

God, teach me to be quiet.
Let me know
The blessedness of silence.
I would go
More calmly on with living.
Though there be
Confusion, lead me, God,
Quietly.

Lucile S. Hull

Self-Portrait

In a loving spirit of generosity a friend once painted my portrait and presented it to me as a special gift. At first I could not bear to look at it. He had emphasized all the flaws of my features, my skin, and the irregular contours of my face. I thought in dismay, "Do I look like *that?* Is that the face everyone sees whenever they're near me?"

I was determined not to hurt my friend's feelings, so I framed the portrait and hung it in the living room where I had to see it every time I walked through. Time passed, and eventually I began to wonder if it was self-love that made me cringe from the brutal truth. I could not accept the flaws I saw that were so painful to me.

But gradually I came to regard the picture for what it is: an honest interpretation of what the artist saw in me, and I humbly admit that my looks leave much to be desired. Little by little I became accustomed to the half-smile the artist gave my mouth and the look of smugness he painted into my expression. Occasionally I look closely at those painted flaws, and like them or not, there they are. But invariably they prompt me to take another look at my inner self. Just as my features are fixed, so is my basic character.

I no longer think of that painting as a portrait of me, but rather the personification of all women who must accept the inevitability of fading hair, wrinkles, sagging chins, and vanishing youth. I am surprised that I can see a new kind of beauty in other women—beauty that has nothing to do with youthfulness, but a kind of inner loveliness. Maybe I, too, can some day project such beauty.

Perhaps there is more in the portrait than the work of an artist. Perhaps the portrait reveals a great depth of understanding of the inner look of the woman who sat for him.

Katherine B. Peavy

Invisible

Illuminating
elusive as starlight
extolled by mystics,
serenity
allured my spirit.
In worship, travel,
in love I sought it,
inquiring, yearning.
Fleetingly
I felt its presence
in someone's gaze,
a sanctuary,
awesome forest.

As I marveled,
always it vanished.

Now alone
in self-made stillness
I meditate.
Wondrously
my spirit seems
peaceful, joyous!
Serenity . . .
no longer sought . . .
embraces me.

Dora J. LaFlamme

We Must Find Peace . . .

Even the hurricane is quiet in the eye
Buried ever so deep in its heart the stillness is found
A nucleus that is mysteriously calm.
Engulfed in the hurry, worry, hubbub of our day
When everyone is flying aimlessly in all directions
Try to find a silence of your own.
Discover your personal bit of inner peace
and cherish every minute.

Tammy Felton

Time and I

the day begins—develops—and ends
time moves on
and i
seem to stand still
     a child is born—matures—and leaves the nest
     time moves on
     and i
     seem to stand still
the wind pounds the beach
the sand moves onto other beaches
time————
and i———————————
     the wind rushes the clouds past
     i see all this happen
     the days coming and going
     the child
     the beach here then gone
     the sky ever changing
     but me————
     time moves on and on
     and i
     seem to stand still

Mary Eleanore Rice

Notes and Rests

This bright morning the heavy quiet of a summer day on our hillside creeps in the open door and envelops me. Only the soft rustle of a leaf and the scolding of a cardinal at an empty feeder break in on my forced solitude. I feel alone.

I know that not far away are the busy thoroughfares of our city, and yet a little distance the many ribbons of intertwining interstate highways. All of these are alive and vibrant with motion of persons, persons, rushing, rushing.

But, sitting here alone, I feel apart and a stranger to the mainstream of living so close by. The mainstream of my life has been damned up into a stagnant pool.

The sound of the birds' songs outside reminds me of the musical orientation of my life—the mass of notes and rests through long hours of practice sessions that were a part of me. I am also thinking of the notes and rests that life brings to each of us.

The notes from the melodies and harmonies, the moving part of our existence, while the rests bring the pauses, the waiting times, when the tempo of our being moves from allegro to andante and finally comes to the rest that life brings to each of us.

Just now I am finding it difficult to make the rests in my life fulfilling and creative.

We have been accused by those in other world cultures of being a nation of activists, a people driven to be in constant motion to find meaning. What then of the times in our life when circumstances slow us down and seem to cut us off from the fresh, free-flowing stream?

Many phrases flood into my thoughts this morning.

"Be still and know."

"Beside restful waters you lead me."

"Wait patiently."

Dear God,
Help me in my struggle. Help me to break down the walls of my aloneness so that I may know oneness with you.

Please assure me that these difficult days of the rest are so ordered by you just as you have set the notes of my life in motion throughout the years.

Help me to know again the vibrancy and purpose of life. Without the rests, the mass of notes would lose their beauty of sound. Help me to find new ways to use these hours creatively as I grow closer to you and more sensitive to those about me. Amen.

Mary Jane Hartman

The Awesomeness of One

"If I could run life through again . . ."
Is surely the saddest
And the silliest
Of all our hypotheses, but—
If I could run life through again
Children would be given one match.
Just one match to start a fire
And thereby they may be taught,
If indeed they *can* be taught
The awesomeness of only one.

Only one grain of corn
Would be put in any hill,
and then that grain tended
With utmost care.
Don't fling five in glad abandon.
One for fire and one for flood,
One for frost and one for greedy crow,
With still another one to grow.
Plant just one that they may know
The terrible awesomeness of one.

And if I could run life through again
I would be compelled
By truth to say
That regardless of how you hold your match,
Despite the way you stare in utter awe
At its endless capabilities,
There may come a storm
With gust so strong,
With such quenching, drenching sheets of rain,
That the brave and valorous little flame
Will gutter,
Flicker
And go out.
There is not immunity
To mortality.

Normagene Warner

Minnie Remembers

God,
My hands are old.
I've never said that out loud before
but they are.
I was so proud of them once.
They were soft
like the velvet smoothness of a firm, ripe peach.
Now the softness is more like wornout sheets
or withered leaves.
When did these slender, graceful hands
become gnarled, shrunken claws?
When, God?
They lie here in my lap,
naked reminders of this worn-out
body that has served me too well!

How long has it been since someone touched me
Twenty years?
Twenty years I've been a widow.
Respected.
Smiled at.
But never touched.
Never held so close that loneliness
was blotted out.

I remember how my mother used to hold me, God.
When I was hurt in spirit or flesh,
she would gather me close,
stroke my silky hair
and caress my back with her warm hands.
O God, I'm so lonely!

I remember the first boy who ever kissed me.
We were both so new at that!
The taste of young lips and popcorn,
the feeling inside of mysteries to come.

I remember Hank and the babies.
How else can I remember them but together?
Out of the fumbling, awkward attempts of new
lovers came the babies.
And as they grew, so did our love.
And, God, Hank didn't seem to mind
if my body thickened and faded a little.

He still loved it. And touched it.
And we didn't mind if we were no longer beautiful.
And the children hugged me a lot.
O God, I'm lonely!

God, why didn't we raise the kids to be silly
and affectionate as well as
dignified and proper?
You see, they do their duty.
They drive up in their fine cars;
they come to my room to pay their respects.
They chatter brightly, and reminisce.
But they don't touch me.
They call me "Mom" or "Mother"
or "Grandma."

> Never Minnie.
> My mother called me Minnie.
> So did my friends.
> Hank called me Minnie, too.
> But they're gone.
> And so is Minnie.
> Only Grandma is here.
> And God! She's lonely!

Donna Swanson

My Private Self

There are things I can't tell others, God,
but I feel safe in telling you.
There are secrets in my heart that none may know.
 Trust is not yet strong enough,
 willingness not great enough—
 I fear they will not understand.
For, I am still in process of becoming.
Daily there emerges from within
 a newer part of me that I must first try out
 before I'm brave enough to share it with the world.
I have a private life, my God,
that belongs to me, to you, and to those special few
before whom I can be just who I am
without fear of judgment or of reprimand.

Alma Roberts

Will I Be?

idly i stand watching people pass by
   as i wonder about my life in fifty years
      will i be absentminded
        weak in the eyes
         slow to walk
     hesitant in my speech
      will i graciously and gently grow in wisdom and in love
       or will i be harsh
         cold
           impatient
      will i seek listeners
     or will i seek to listen
   will i have physical health
        and spiritual malnutrition
   will i have the stench of sour milk
     or the sweet fragrance of a rose
      the choice is mine

Penny Tressler

Work and Service

Integrity

If I am salt,
I am essence.
Dilute, I am nothing.
If the salt of me is dissolved and washed away,
it leaves an emptiness in me
and a cast of bitter crystals
        where it dries.

My essence—
I must keep it whole.
If I am false to me, and to you,
my strength dissolves and runs
        in easy rivulets to sea
            to join the waves that beat
                against the shore.
There will be naught to stand
            where I have stood.

Integrity is strained by easy temptings that rain over me,
by storms that strike the spirit
        of my wholeness.
Down on my knees I ask God's help.
Only by remaining whole can I survive
            and serve.
   Prayer: Dear God, help me, please, to recognize the storms that
would destroy my spirit so that I can fortify myself to serve you.
Amen.

Elinor J. George

Not for the Hesitant

It is a daring prayer: "Thy will be done!"
If answered, it might well destroy our ways.
There may be heights where we are called to run
With victory eluding all our days.
But cautious prayers produce such timid souls,
And dreams can die while waiting for their time.
My hands might never touch the high-set goals;
Yet I must stake my life upon the climb.

Hazel Nowell Ailor

A Call to Worship and a Prayer

Sisters and Brothers—Arise!
Arise and lift your hearts
Arise and lift your eyes
Arise and lift your voices.

The living God,
The living, moving Spirit of God
has called us together—
in witness
in celebration
in struggle.

Reach out toward each other.
Our God reaches out toward us!

Let us worship God!

Spirit of God—Holy God, Wind of God, Fire of God, Life of God—
Anoint us to be a people of your Good News, yoke to break yokes,
sighted to bring sight, healed to be healers, struggling to bring release.
 Shower us and comfort us in the shining light and darkness of your
glorious mystery. We invoke *your* mystery, not ours. We invoke *your*
clarity, not ours. We invoke *your* truth, not ours.
 Spirit of God—Holy God, Wind of God, Fire of God, Life of God—
you who made Deborah and Miriam, Mary and Dorcas, Joan of Arc,
Sojourner Truth, and Rosa Parks cry out through the Cosmos, cry out
through us. Make your justice, your work, and your love real through
our lives. Amen.

Elizabeth Rice

Jesus, Friend of Women

Jesus, friend of women,
We turn to you today;
We long for health and wholeness
And love to light our way.
The woman of Samaria
Was not cast off by you,
But gained new life unending.
Give us that new life, too!

You healed the stricken woman,
Raised Jairus' girl to life,
Made sinful men stop stoning,
Bid each man love his wife.
The perfumed oil you cherished,
The marriage feast you shared;
Like us, you wept in sorrow,
And children knew you cared.

Like Martha, we are burdened,
With household chores confined,
But we would be like Mary
And serve you with the mind.
O living Christ, to women
That first glad Easter day
You came in risen glory;
So come to us, we pray.

O Jesus, through all the ages
You've tried to set us free.
With women saints, and prophets
You've shared your ministry.
From ancient forms now free us,
Show us new ways to live,
New ways to love your people
And share the life you give.

Betsy Phillips Fisher

This, Too, Is Discipleship

A kind of martyrdom, tiredness:
    (I didn't communicate and should have)
But without heroics.

Come. Listen. Impale yourself
    on the sculpted memorials
        of anecdotes which,
            relegated to memory,
               seem
                    innocent.

No one will see your bleeding. They're
Dealing with feelings
Of rising refusal
To answer requests
To attend
Regularly
Scheduled
Meetings.

Mary Frances Palmer

A Dream

I dream of
A new kind of bishop
Breath of spring in the sameness of solemn black
Dancing bishop in bright liturgical caftan
Breaking for communion the bread she has baked
Visiting oppressed nations as one who knows what it means to be
    oppressed
A mother figure to her ministers
Ordaining young women and also young men
Singing, acting out a sermon
Nurturing the church to communicate God's love
Writing, speaking in a fresh idiom
A new prophetic voice for the freedom of all people.

Sue Ralph

Anyplace Can Be Home

Ten moves in twenty years,
The corporate gypsy life.
We are counted among the one in five American families who move
    each year.
From the heart of America to the South, then to New York, to Cali-
    fornia, to our nation's capital, to New England, even Southeast Asia
    and Micronesia.
Anyplace can be home in God's world.

An apartment, hotel, house, trailer—wherever the family is together.
    It is sharing and the caring that makes the difference.
Adjustments to be made—new customs, new job personnel, new
    friends to make.
We must take nothing for granted.
There are no relatives or old friends to love and accept us in each new
    place.
All kinds of changes must be made at once. We must keep trying.
It is not easy.
But anyplace can be home in God's world.

We find a sense of mission in this way of life.
God is with us wherever we are. We are God's children, in God's world.
We have learned to appreciate diversity in people.
There is an adventure in new places and different ways, awareness in
    nature and changes we see.
We are always learning. And understanding—or trying.
And sharing. It works both ways.
Anyplace can be home in God's world.

There is one consistency in all our moves.
The fellowship of Christ.
It is always there—sometimes small, sometimes large.
It is our anchor in each new community.
People who care make all the difference.
And there are opportunities for service in all places.
The mobile life is not all bad.
In fact it is very good.
For anyplace can be home in God's world.

Marianne Jewell

Seeker

God, my world is out of balance, and the tension hurts.
Who am I?
What am I doing here?

Your Word comes to me from every side and I stand
in confusion before this maelstrom of opportunity.
Can I not escape?
Retreat into the safe anonymity of everyday necessity?

You say "Speak!" when my tongue stammers to a halt.
You say "Love!" as I shrink back into my portable shell.

Is this woman who lives in here
Mother?
Wife?
Daughter?
or is she Christian?
Seeker?
Leader?

"The same skin can hold them both," you say.
Ridiculous!

Who can concentrate on seeking with an eyeful of oatmeal
And a lapful of squirming humanity!

Who do I lead with no formal training?
No background of "correct" requirements?
Have I the right?
Isn't there danger of leading them astray?
O God, I can think of so many excuses!

But the Word is still there.
It will not let me go.
It fills my life.
It invades my world.
I am surprised by love
and compelled by joy to speak.

So be it
I am Woman.
I am Christian.
I am Seeker.

But best of all, my God, I am your beloved child!

Donna Swanson

Get the Action Started

Women of the twentieth century—what is our mission today? Perhaps it has not changed through the years, but our concept of it has changed. Our stress in this twentieth century has been humanity—the worth of the human individual—people! Before we can be effective in ministry, we will need to know who we are, or perhaps whose we are, and then we can discover what we are to become. When we know who we are, then we can become women in mission.

Who am I? I am a child of God, a human being, a unique individual in the eyes of God. I cannot be like Mother wanted me to be, or what Father wanted me to become—because I am myself. I realize that I must continually seek to discover myself with the help of God.

Part of self-discovery is self-identity. I am a woman. Am I ready to prepare myself to face the good news of liberation for women? I think the fact that we are now considering *peoplehood* and *personhood* to be a more complete word than *brotherhood* is good. I am certain that women, as a whole, want liberation for women and men. We are struggling for the day when society can look upon "people" as beautiful because they are human; the day when each woman and each man feel freedom from societal pressures that release them from conformity of stereotyped roles because of their sex. Liberation, to me, is freedom to be and freedom to become.

One of our missions then as women of the twentieth century is to help open the door of understanding to people—to help them become full persons. When we have determined who we are and what our place in the world is, then total liberation can become a reality. Our first assignment is to be ourselves, to stop playing roles, and to realize that we are individual human beings who need people and who can help people. Our mission extends beyond helping the old, the young, a different race, but to helping middle-class Americans as well.

Second, we women have a mission to choose priorities in this twentieth century. It is a time when people power and women power can accomplish many things. It is a time, though, of so much activity that we are pulled in every direction. We have many crises in the world—war, poverty, population explosion, pollution, to name a few. We have many national problems of the same caliber. We are concerned about injustices, discrimination, legislation. We are concerned also in state and county and community. The world has become smaller and what affects someone or some people miles away can also affect us. And yet, we find we are pressured locally by the status quo.

We know as people that we are called to be both "Marthas" and "Marys," and both are necessary sometimes. But to be effective missioners, we must choose priorities, do effectively what we are required to do in our chosen mission, and not worry about what "they" will think if we do not participate in something that someone else thinks is important. Each woman must choose for herself where she can best serve and where she can use her particular potential to serve people to the fullest and to enjoy her personhood.

Joy Uthoff

You Must Mean Something Else

God, me a minister?
It can't be—
I'm a woman—
You must mean something else.

I have a husband
and five children.
I'm a woman—
You must mean something else.

I'll be glad to work in the church
To sing, type, or teach
But—God, not preach—
You must mean something else.

God, I'm trying to really listen
Have gone through so much in my life—
So much toil, so much strife—
You must mean something else.

My husband is good and kind.
The kids are great, they're really fine.
But go to school for such a long time?
You must mean something else.

There are so many with so much need
I must listen to your heed.
Because I'm a woman—
Must you mean something else?

Lydia Saenz

Prison

Many of us are creatively imprisoned because we choose to be.
Designating the warden to be ourselves,
we allow (sometimes encourage) fear to shackle our God-given gift
        of creativity.
    The mere thought
of doing something "new" or "different"
    sends us scurrying
    to the darkest corner of our cell
    voluntarily placing ourselves
    in solitary confinement.
    Meanwhile—
God the gracious, creative Governor
    seeks to grant a pardon if we will but receive it.

Penny Tressler

~

Until woman assumes
her rightful place
in Christian ministry,
Christ has only one hand
with which to heal
to strengthen,
to touch,
and
to console.

Sr. Martha Ann Kirk

The Future

Amen, Sister!

Jesus used this word many times,
   putting his stamp of approval,
   giving his confirmation or agreement.
We forget! Or are we fearful of
   being thought "square"?

Maybe we need more Amens.
Maybe we need to hear
   and experience more of life
   to which we can say Amen.
Tonight my heart and mind throbs with *Amens.*

For new ways of service
   for new thinking,
   creative ideas,
   new listening to the World Out There,
   for friends old and new.
Amen, Sister!

For the stimulation of young women,
For the puzzlement of new machines and new humanities,
For the discovery of people in all parts of the world.
Amen, Sister!

For the invitation from Matthew
   to follow a teacher not like others.
For being a woman in a changing world,
   especially a Christian woman capable of growth toward new
      maturity in Christ.
For all of this and more!
Amen, Sister! Hallelujah!

Pauline Reeder Liddle

~

Journeying is more
Than reaching destinations.
Journeying is more.

Jean Fox Holland

On Being Born Again

The mind contracts.
The senses tighten
and I am thrust forward,
propelled into new birth.

The self within groans to be born,
struggles to free itself
from the bands
of fetal insecurity.

Vainly I shrink back from knowing,
blindly brush aside the
blurred images
of a new beginning.

Torn between helpless rage
and burning curiosity,
I walk the limbo of
each day's necessity.

No matter that others
have stood here.
Each birth is isolated
in its terror and expectation.

Their brave words mock me.
Their success reveals
only my failure.
They are aliens in my world.
Wait for me!
I'm coming!

Donna Swanson

On the Edge of Time

On the Edge of Time

Between the known of my past:
    People I can hardly bear to leave behind,
    A job I know exactly how to handle,
    A home that is a nest of security,
              and
The vast unknown of the future ahead:
    People to work with and live with whom I will need to learn to love
        and trust,
    A job that seems almost unbelievably demanding of my talents and
        my time,
    A home—I don't even know where my home will be.

Why do I feel I must go through this door?
Because God calls me!

      All these years I've prayed that I could serve God in whatever I
        did.
      Now God's opened this new door for this phase of my life,
        so I must go.
      Risking, sacrificing, leaving behind,
        crying—I must go.

      As I grew in my relationship with God,
      I finally had the courage to say
      "Take my life and do with it what you will."
      Now God's opened this new door,
        so I must go.
      Expecting, hoping, adventuring, trusting,
        I must go.

How in the world will I manage?
Because I can believe!

      Believing in the God whose will is wholeness,
      Believing in the Christ who will guide me on the journey,
      Believing in the Holy Spirit who gives us each the power to do
        more than we can believe or dare to ask for,

      Believing all this,
      I step
          across the edge of time
             through the door into the future
On my journey to wholeness in Christ.

Martha Edens

. . . *Every New Day I Have a New Chance*

After struggling to choose an answer to the question of what is most precious in my life, I believe I now see it clearly: Most precious to me is the assurance of the grace of God—and its availability! To me this means

> that God loves me when I least deserve to be loved
>
> that God accepts me—as I am—in so many ways unacceptable
>
> that God forgives me—again and again—when I fall short of my commitments
>
> that every new day I have a chance—a fresh start—to try again.

> It is this grace which gives me the courage (and endows me with some skill) to attempt to do more than I am able to do, and to become more than I can ever become.

God's grace frees me to dare and to risk.

Margaret L. Sonnenday

Mary in Me

Virgin in me
has harbored the expectation
of miracles
I have felt the beating of the dove's wings
Mother in me
has celebrated the ecstasy
of being earth
I have held creation at my breast

Mary in me
has shuddered in the terror
of amazement
I have been known by God

Woman in me
has been afraid in the shimmering light
of a winter moon
I have waited

Come, Morning Star

Virginia Olsen White

Choice

The choice is made.
The agony of choosing done.
Yes to one possibility is
No forever to that other way.
But the turmoil does not cease.
I stand alone with my choice
Freely made. My future now unsure.
The security of that not chosen gone.

I fear some are hurt by my choosing
And that weighs my spirit down.
My ears ring with a bitter voice,
"Well, I hope you got what you wanted."

My God, are you in the choosing?
I do not know.
You are so silent.
You are silent far too long.

I yearn for peace
   And you challenge me.
I yearn for answers
   And you pose questions.
I yearn to know the right
   And you send choices.
It was easier before I knew my freedom.
I was that tiny blind girl
Led safely, shielded, coddled by those who wished me blind.
I did not bother to let them know it was pretend.

But I grow as I choose.
I feel the joy and the pain of choice.
I do not need little girl coddling.
In my tears and frailty, I feel new strength
For I alone have chosen.
And I only trust it was the faithful choice.
Forgive me, merciful God, for my unfaithfulness
And help me grow through the new choice of today.

Mary Anne Morefield

The Future Breaking In

It's more than that, you know.

More than deciding
who opens the door
who chairs the committee
who waxes the floor

or allowing the woman to speak
in a sacred place.

The vision
is just stirring in the shell
and requires a tearing,
a breaking up of pieces,
a release from the past.

The vision
is Woman
turning into a woman
and Man
turning into a man
who'd rather care than compete
who spend some time listening
who write "sister" or "brother"
instead of "Dear Sir":

who give up their life for each other
feeding
healing
touching

forgetting that one was called great
and one was called nothing—

people free to need each other

in the unity
of one Spirit

where each person is the Gift
and the Giver

and no one goes without a name.

Greta Schumm

The Reality of the Future

As I free my mind to wander, unrestrained, moving at will with freedom of choice, I see visions of unfolding events, much to my liking and much planned for my good. The future looks bright in the course of a dream. I venture forth seeing life as it could be, not knowing the course ahead, but picturing it as though I did. I see that which reality denies me, beautifully designed by my own invention for the purpose of enriching my future destiny.

I pass by the testings and hardships, the painful experiences of growing. I see no element uninvited or unwanted. I omit the times of frustration and struggle. The dark side, the low side does not exist in my wandering dreamworld at all. I am free as I float in this blissful ecstasy of illusion.

But, dear God, guide me back to the state of reality. Help me not to hide from life. I know that I cannot remain in my dreamworld, but I thank you for the capacity of being able to float about in this way. I give you thanks that you have presented life to me in its fullness. Although I can never fully understand, I place my hope, my trust in you. Bring my dreamworld into the fullness of reality, containing all elements of life, consecrated to your will.

Joan Moore

Benediction

Sisters and brothers, Rise for the benediction
Grasp the hands of the persons on either side of you

Go forth in the name of the living, caring God
who by nature is female and male

Go forth to hear the wisdom in the stories
of our foremothers and forefathers

Go forth to confront all that enslaves
the spirits of children, women, and men

and,
Go forth rejoicing that we have each other
for the renewal of our spirits.

AMEN.

Phyllis Tyler Wayman

The Journey

where are you going i asked
to places i have never been
was the answer
what do you plan to do i asked
my purpose will be evident at journey's end
who has planned your itinerary i asked
its plan will be revealed at times most unlikely
why would you consent to such a vague plan i said
i accepted the challenge
when i accepted life was the answer

Mary Eleanore Rice

Metamorphoses

Becoming a butterfly
    dwarfs the used cocoon.
There is no going back,
    no lessening of spaces
    for those wings.
Remembered comfort calls occasionally
    when storms blow near.
But wings require
    the room for soaring.
Wings gleam with future,
    not with memory.
Without a turning backward,
    wings may take
    a butterfly to green, fresh fields,
    undreamed of yet.
The longing
    for a warm cocoon recedes
    as new worlds beckon
    eager butterflies.

Hazel Nowell Ailor

Flight

I am bird frail
    fluttering on the rim of straw
    knowing that a fall
    may be instantly fatal.

My untried wings
    test airs with fear
    slicing the clouds
    to find security.

I am hovering here
    cautiously
    above daisies and stones
    looking at downs and sinking.

If I dared trust
    the tiny infinite hollows of feathers
    to brace me up
    I'd soar into the sun.

Is there strength enough in grace?
Is the secure swoop possible even for me?

I will give my life to it!

AWAY

UPWARD

GLIDE THE WIND!

Sara Covin Juengst

Index